I WAS CHOSEN TO MAKE IT

I Was Chosen to Make It

BY ALEXANDRA HELENE

Palmetto Publishing Group
Charleston, SC

First Edition

Printed in the United States

Paperback: 978-1-64111-759-3
Hardback: 978-1-64111-758-6
eBook: 978-1-64111-937-5

For my Grandmother, Irene. You saved me.

Prologue

I'M SITTING ON A BENCH IN THE HARBOR OF SAN Francisco, staring across the bay at Alcatraz Island. There stands a vacant home on an unforgiving rock for misguided souls. I imagine part of their daily torture was to look out upon that same bay and see people like me enjoying their freedom—laughing, playing, and taking sweet sun-filled afternoon naps beneath trees blossoming in the spring shade.

I lived most of my life on a self-created Alcatraz of sorts, in a constant state of isolation and despair, of which there was no wiggle room for escape. My prison bars wrapped around me like a steel blanket. I didn't want anyone to touch me out of fear that my poison would invade their veins and course through them like salt, for my blood was dirty, contaminated with self-loathing, shame, anxiety, and anger. I stood untouchable, unremarkable, uncomfortable, and unsettled, encased within a set of bars I had built around myself. I hated myself. I hated who I had become.

I had no idea how it all happened or why I allowed so many people to decide who I was. I was a thief, a liar, a homewrecker, and a whore. I was stupid, worthless, average, spoiled, and bratty. I was intolerable, irritable, bitchy, cold, and heartless. And I believed all of it, spending countless years of my life either living up to those labels, or fighting them in any way possible. I would prove everyone right or everyone wrong, according to the role they played in whatever scene that I had created.

As I sit here staring across the water at Alcatraz Island, I envision ghosts of people there just like me, out of control of their thoughts and actions, which would then lead them to rebel, fight, and ultimately land themselves locked in a cage. I allowed people to do that to me. I permitted people to tell me who I was. It was my fault.

PART I

One

A YEAR AGO, YOU WOULD HAVE NEVER FOUND ME sitting on a park bench alone in an unknown city. I knew there was a bridge here, a lot of fog, and a prison on a rock. San Francisco, as far as I knew, was the land of earthquakes, hippies, trolley cars, and sky-high rent. I would have been at home on my couch in a constant state of self-induced loneliness, although not alone by any means. I had a lovely house, two beautiful luxury cars, four gregarious children, and a husband who took more bullshit from me than one person should ever have in a lifetime. He loved me, and I didn't care.

For nearly twenty years, he loved me, and I didn't care. I didn't care about my friends, my house, or my cars and scarcely seemed to care much about my kids. I did the mom thing. I went to school functions, recitals, and concerts and drove them all over town. The *mom thing* went just fine, but that was the extent of my parenting. I was there but not present. I was too busy getting my joy from a bottle. I loved my children absolutely, but I just saw them as four massive moving pieces of endless work and responsibility. As a young mother, I had just gone through the motions instead of the emotions. I didn't have those.

I'm relatively sure that at some point I did, but I shut down soon after my first fight-or-flight response was activated. My first memory: I was three years old and asleep in my bed when I heard yelling and the sound of things crashing. I crept down the stairs in my Holly Hobbie nightgown and sat with my face squished between the wrought iron rails. My mom was in her robe and slippers, crouched behind the quartersawn rocking chair in the living room. She was crying in her hands. My dad was in the kitchen, picking up and smashing things against the walls and floor. The lamps in the living room crashed, tables upended, and pictures ripped from the walls. My mother caught sight of me and whispered, "Go back to bed." Instead, I ran down to her, and she scooped me into her arms, trying to hide me. Three-year-old me sat there stoic and unafraid. I would tell my dad to leave her alone, but of course I didn't. Mom said she was ok and that I had better get back in my bed before Dad saw me.

The next thing I knew, my baby brother, Mom, and I were in my grandparents' car, headed to their house. I don't know how long we stayed at grandma's house, but when we went back home, Mom opened the front door to see the house exactly as we left it. Everything was in pieces, including my mom and I. I noticed that the jar where my mom kept my reward lollipops was smashed, and the candy was spilled all over the floor. As my mom grabbed the broom and dustpan to start cleaning up the wreckage, I grabbed as many lollipops as I could (the green ones, because I liked those the best) and hid them behind the couch where I would go to eat them over the next few days.

Two

I GREW UP IN THE NEW JERSEY SUBURBS AS THE oldest child in a family of five. On the outside, we were the typical '80s family. Dire Straits, The Who, and Bruce Springsteen often blared out of the stereo on Saturday mornings. Mom played racquetball and brunched with the girls. We lived in a small wood-shingled Cape Cod–style house built in the 1950s. It nestled itself on a small tree-lined street of just seven little houses just like ours, and I was the only girl on the block.

I was as tomboy as a girl could be. As my mom's only girl, I had a pale-pink bike with a yellow and pink-flowered banana seat and streamers flowing from the handlebars. The dainty Huffy two-wheeler also had a giant white basket and finger bell. You'd always find me trailing behind the neighborhood boys as they cruised down the streets on their fancy BMX and Mongoose trick bikes, popping wheelies and dreaming about turning Freddie's side yard into a dirt bike track. The three of them wanted to be like their idol, David Baily, American Motocross Champion of 1984.

It was the '80s after all, when kids were still allowed to be kids. We dashed out the door at dawn, came home for a bologna and cheese sandwich when our stomachs reminded us to eat, and came home when we heard our mothers bellowing our names from the front door, calling us for dinner. We tumbled in tired, dirty, and happy.

I was a self-proclaimed one of the boys and did my damnedest to be one of them. If I dressed like them, spoke like them, and spit on the sidewalk like them, I could blend in with no problem. Those boys were my friends, my real friends, and my only friends. They were full of excitement and curiosity and encompassed the very definition of freedom. I wanted that, too, and I had it for the most part. I assimilated just fine until a new girl with pretty blond pigtails and big brown eyes moved in across the street, throwing a massive wrench into how I saw myself.

Weeks later, I was the flower girl dressed in a mock wedding between Katie and Freddie. All of our parents came with their smiles and clicking cameras. My five-year-old self stood there in a long yellow chiffon dress that belonged to Katie's teenage sister, Jenny, and was about ten sizes too big.

I remember wanting to be Katie. I wanted to be the one Freddie was marrying. I didn't even like Freddie in that way, but even so, my little brain wondered why I wasn't the one. Wasn't I just as cute as Katie? What was wrong with me? Maybe I had made myself too much of a tomboy, and the boys didn't see me as a girl. After the exchanging of aluminum foil rings on the top step of Freddie's front porch, I walked back next door to my house, tripping on my dress the entire way. In my room I collapsed in a heap, tears of my first heartbreak stinging my chunky, freckled cheeks.

After I collected myself, I went back outside and opened the chain-linked gate that led to our backyard. I sat crisscross applesauce under the plum tree, heavy with its bright-pink blossoms. I started to feel something boiling up inside of me. It was jealousy, and I didn't like feeling this way. That boiling was anger rising into my chest and lighting a fire. Katie had what I wanted. How could I be one of the boys and be seen as a girl too? Was that even a thing? I thought I had to be one or the other. Identifying as both genders would confuse everyone and probably make my parents mad.

I just couldn't be me, whatever I was. I felt different from the other girls I saw. I wasn't prissy or frilly. I didn't want painted nails or long waving ribbons in my hair. I wore ripped pants, Zips sneakers, and my hair pulled back in a messy ponytail held by a rubber band. When I came home with scraped knees and dirt on my face from hanging with the neighborhood boys all day, it was right into the bath with me. Any trace of masculinity went down the tub drain with my friend, Mr. Bubble. Into my pretty little nightgown I would slip, with hair set up in curlers for the next school day.

I didn't fit in at school either. By first grade, I had felt like a square peg trying to fit into a round hole. My two best pals were Kelly and Vinny. Kelly was in ballet school with me, and she always wore long-trailing beaded ribbons in her hair. She had a small mole that sat just below her left eye. I thought Kelly looked like a movie star. She wore a dress to school every day and had a pair of socks to match each one. I don't think Kelly owned a pair of Zips because all she ever had on her feet were black-and-white saddle shoes that were always freshly polished and unscuffed. She sat at her desk in perfect posture, with her feet crossed at the ankles and her hands folded in her lap. Kelly was the picture-perfect mold of a seven-year-old girl. She got noticed. The attention she got from all the boys in our class sparked more feelings of jealousy. Kelly was pretty, smart, and funny. I was just awkward.

While Kelly sat on the blacktop and played jacks, I spent my recesses running and stomping my way through pigweed fields and sand, trying to catch Vinny. Vinny was small and fast, had bright-green eyes, and loved the Miami Dolphins. The heavy gold cross that anchored itself around Vinny's neck broke as I grabbed him by the shirt collar the day that I finally caught him.

"Hey! My uncle gave me that cross for my Holy Communion, and now it's *lost*," he yelled. He marched right past me and up to our teacher. Ms. Decker called home and informed my parents that not only had I broken Vinny's necklace but that I had spent my lunch-time chasing boys. I only wanted Vinny's attention, and I got it all right. He hated me the rest of the school year, and Mom and Dad asked me why I felt the need to chase boys around. It was because they weren't chasing me. I wasn't Kelly any more than I was Katie.

Three

MY BROTHER AND I SPENT MOST OF OUR TIME AT home navigating our father's unpredictable moods and my mother's fear of them. After having a front-row seat to that mess of a fight between my parents years prior, I had learned when to stay out of my father's way. I knew when to get away and hide as quickly as possible if the barometer started to dip. My brother, however, was prone stick around and poke the bear. Quite often he would push our father so far that he'd be jumping across the table and chasing him down over something as small as a spilled bowl of soup.

I was the smart one. By ten years old, I had been able to tell when Dad was going to blow. Sometimes Mom would clue us in by telling us he had a bad day at work or too much money had been spent. Her instructions were just to clear out and scatter. The worst of my dad's moods arrived after the end of *summer camp*, the National Guard's two weeks of duty in the late summer. We got the very worst of Dad then. I hid in my room for days to avoid his volcanic flow. Once that lava started to ooze down that mountain, you had better get the hell out of the way or burn up in anger right along with him.

I don't want to paint my homelife as a house of eternal horror. My parents did the best they could with what their parents had given them. I knew my grandparents as well as any kid could, but there was no telling where they came from any more than you could tell where the ZZ Top–looking bearded guy, who loitered outside of the local Quik Check, was raised. My parents rarely talked about their upbringing, aside from how good I had it compared to them.

I had a little bit of insight once from my grandmother in one of her infamous living room chats that she enjoyed having with me from time to time. She'd sit in her Ethan Allan powder-blue recliner, feet up with hands across her belly, telling stories from the Depression, about her five brothers, and what life was like growing up the only girl to two Russian immigrants who spoke broken English.

Mom's mother always had stories and heartfelt advice, but one of the most striking things she ever told me was "When you grow up and have your own family, be sure you tell your kids you love them because I never told mine." That explained my mother in a nutshell. As for my father, I knew even less. What I did know was that it was better to be kicked by him under the dinner table for swinging my legs than it was to have a porcelain dinner plate cracked over my head when I spoke without having been asked to speak. My Dad's mother always complained about us kids, and my grandfather would tell her, "Leave the kids alone, Edna Mae." And Edna Mae would leave us alone. Meanwhile, I was sweat stuck to the plastic-covered couch, popping M&Ms into my mouth trying to keep quiet out of fear of being sent to the self-proclaimed haunted upstairs.

My parents were good people. They are good people. I always got the feeling they were people trapped by circumstance. They didn't know what they didn't know. Mom was always there for my dance competitions and recitals, putting my hair up in tight ballet buns and painting my face with Covergirl, and Dad was always there to soothe broken hearts. They didn't do so well on the huge things—the pivotal, life-changing, monumental, deep pains and mistakes of growing up and all the trouble that went along with it. When it came to that stuff, they had no idea what to do, and I don't fault them for that.

How can you give away something you don't have? It's like asking a tree to pick up and move when it's perfectly comfortable where it is. It has just the right amount of sun and shade, has adequate water, and the cold weather doesn't bother it too much. The roots run deep, and it will either bloom beautifully year after year where it has been planted or succumb to drought and disease, but it will never move a single day in its entire life.

I like to think that people are very much like trees. Some are healthy, sturdy, and majestic as oaks. Others can be more fragile and need more care like fruits. Some still come back fighting even after multiple attempts to cut them back or cut them down. Roots again sprout up through the dirt and keep trying to survive. I'm that third type of tree, fighting and clawing its way through thick layers of earth and muck, struggling to grow up and outward, yearning to be that old giant shade tree that harbors the life beneath it.

Four

DEFEATED AND AFRAID IS A GREAT WAY TO DEFINE much of my life. The roots of my tree entwined with the roots of other trees. I had no idea where their origin stopped and mine began. Who the hell was I anyway, aside from just a sum of moving parts? Parts that had been collected over the years and assembled haphazardly.

Bits and pieces of everyone I knew and loved banged around inside of me, disjointed and metallic. I took parts of people willingly, squirreling them away for safekeeping, never knowing when that piece would be of use. I was but a mere collection of other people's thoughts, ideas, words, and opinions that slowly rose through my roots and out into my branches like a slow poison.

With all of those jumbled-up pieces, I was always very well put together. I could stop traffic with my looks and melt an entire room with my wit and charm, never bringing to the table anything less than my best. I was loud, in charge, immeasurable, unstoppable, accessible, and found at the top of every heap because I worked my ever-living ass off to climb there. Get in my way and you'll be run over by a force so intense you'll be left raw and aching for days. I was strong and beautiful with children to match and a husband as doting and committed as they come. I was the picture-perfect mom, wife, and upstanding citizen in my community. Nobody knew from looking at me that I was an alcoholic.

Becoming an alcoholic isn't something that happens overnight. Nobody goes to bed at night and wakes up in the morning a drunk. It is something that develops over time, unnoticed until it's there, pummeling you in the face as you watch the wheels of your life detach and start rolling down the hill. You can try and catch those wheels, but they will just keep gaining momentum the further they roll. You'll never catch up until they are sitting in a pile at the bottom of the hill with you sitting in the middle of the steaming heap of burnt-up rubber, wondering what the hell happened to your life. That's alcoholism.

I must have lost control somewhere. How else could my life be such a mess? I had convinced myself that I was fine, everything was fine, and I was managing just fine. But it wasn't fine. In the end, I had lost nearly everything I had ever loved. My father raised me to be tough, and that's what I convinced myself I was. Time after time, I'd walk down to the bottom of that hill, gather up my burnt-up tires, and put them back on my bus.

Five

EVERYONE HAS A STORY, BUT VERY FEW ARE WILL-ing to tell it in the way it should be told—with bravery, honesty, and truth. Allowing yourself to be completely vulnerable isn't easy. It opens you up to criticism, ridicule, and potential life-altering back-lash by calloused hands.

Exposing yourself as a human being to another human being takes courage. It's a treasure for the world's most broken as a means to heal, and that takes work that is deep-digging, soul-searching, bone-crushing, and pain-ridden. This type of healing is not for the people who need it, because true healing comes at a price. You must throw out your person as you know it, in exchange for one that you have never seen before. True healing is for those who want it more than they've ever wanted anything else.

Getting drunk was a hell of a lot easier. Who in their right mind would want to discover, learn, accept, and repair their boiling-up insides? The desperate. The people with nothing left to lose. The people who had found their rock bottom had a basement, and there was no ladder or elevator back up to the surface. There was only a shovel propped up against the wall so you could go down even further.

The easier way is the drunk way. It's the complete checking out, the avoidance, the darkness, and the pretending. Throw some alcohol on top and worry about it tomorrow, but the tomorrows keep coming, and I found that there wasn't nearly enough chardonnay. There are too many tomorrows if you can't bring yourself to let go of all of the yesterdays.

I could not let go of anything. Yesterdays are always alive in my head, playing on an endless loop. I can even remember the exact pair of socks I wore to school on the first day of kindergarten. I can remember faces, dates, places, birthdays, battles, and victories, but mostly I remember the people who did me wrong. It was a dark and twisted life goal of mine to get my revenge, to make them as miserable and hurt as I was. I was determined to have the last say and the last laugh, and the biggest grin would be on my face as I watched everything come crashing down around them. If I could get you before you got to me, even better. Terrified children become angry, resentful, spiritually sick children, walking around in adult bodies who often find themselves in the hole of an addiction or an ism.

Alcohol is an amazing off switch for a brain that doesn't have one. If I didn't want to think or feel, it was my salvation. If someone made me mad, the kids were irritating, or I was fighting with my husband, I'd have a drink. If there was a birthday party, a girl's night, or a date night, I was having drinks. If it was raining or snowing, or there was football on TV, I was drinking. I drank when I was happy, sad, angry, lonely, tired, nostalgic, relaxed, uncomfortable, anxious, or excited. I lifted my glass in honor of the dead, new babies, new jobs, getting fired, anniversaries, and divorces. The only divorce I didn't drink to was my own, for it was liquor that had brought it to my doorstep.

Alcohol is the great remover of all things. It removes jobs, friends, and families. It not only removes those awful feelings of worthlessness and misery but erases every moment of joy too. I may have chosen to drink, but in the end, the drink chose me and tightened its grip until every last thing that was good in my life was extinguished. It was as if a match had been struck and thrown carelessly to the ground, and all that would remain from the blazing inferno were piles of soot left for the wind to scatter. You'd think I would have known better. I had a front-row seat to the show of the explosive and unpredictable insanity of alcoholism, and the tickets were expensive.

Six

MY VERY FIRST MEMORY AS A KID WAS VIOLENCE. IT chiseled itself on the blank slate of who I was and got carried around like a book under my arm. Every wrong moment, every little hiccup, and every misfortune got written down, and slowly I became everything but the vision God had intended. I was the summation of opinions, perceptions, and circumstances. I was a victim. I didn't put myself into a position to be hurt initially. Having no tools to deal with what had happened nor the brain maturity to comprehend anything beyond what I saw at the surface, a little girl began to hurt and didn't know what to do about it aside from turning it inward. The only thing I knew was to stuff hurtful things inside of my body like a storage unit. I gathered people's ideas of me and became those ideas. Words became labels, and labels became truth.

The first memory imprinted—violence by my father while nestled in the crook of my mother's arm—and every perception was changed. From age three, my brain had classified men as violent and unpredictable. They were mysterious, larger-than-life creatures that I had to hide from to keep safe, and then the year I learned how to tie my shoes and count to one hundred, someone else picked up the chisel and signed his name to my slate.

My father insisted we all go to Sunday school every single Sunday. When I asked him why we had to go all the time, he blankly said, "It's just what we do. End of discussion." And so I went, not that there was any choice. Whatever my dad said I was convinced had been written as a law in a book that lined the shelves in a massive library somewhere.

Sunday school was the place where we praised the Lord, danced in our seats, examined our shoes at prayer time, dropped our nickels in the collection plate, and all of the teachers were a million years old. I remember the pastor of the church, whose name was Sauerwine, and I always thought about all those misfortunate people up at the altar every Sunday drinking sour wine.

Mom always dressed me up fancy each Sunday. I could never figure out why God cared about what I looked like, but I suppose if you're going to someone's house, you should look presentable to the host. I wore dresses with lacy white gloves and patent leather shoes. I wore itchy pink ankle socks and had brightly colored ribbons cascading down my thick auburn hair that my father had painstakingly washed, dried, and set the night before. Dense freckles dotted my button nose that sat below a pair of light-ocean-blue eyes, and a toothless pasted-on grin completed my polished parade look.

One morning as the words to "I Will Make You Fishers of Men" floated out of my mouth, I caught an eighth-grade boy staring at me from his rusting metal folding chair across the fellowship hall. Every time I looked up from the song sheet I couldn't yet read, a twisted grin shot in my direction, making me squirm in my seat. That day, during our short recess time, he came up to me at the swings and asked me what my name was. When my feet found the ground, he squatted down to where my eyes could meet his and told me to put out my hand. When I did, a shiny new quarter appeared in my palm. "You can put this in the collection plate today or keep it for yourself."

The next Sunday, he turned around to look at me just as he had done the week before. He noticed that I was flipping a quarter around in my hand. At the swings that day, he came to ask me if that was his quarter. I didn't say anything. This time, he put two quarters in my hand. Now I had enough money to buy my favorite blueberry Hubba Bubba bubble gum, but that Hubba Bubba wound up costing me far more than fifty cents.

He liked that I wore dresses. Dresses meant that he could touch me on the bottom underneath them. Sitting on his lap during snack time made my tummy flip over, but I was getting quarters, and nobody said anything about the five-year-old squirming around uncomfortably on the lap of a teenage boy. When I finally worked up the courage to tell Mom about this boy at Sunday school, she looked at me with hands on her hips and said, "Well, that's a great story." Mom didn't believe me.

I ran up to my room and brought down my squirreled quarters to show her. "What are these for, and where did they come from?" she asked. I looked down at my shoes and told her that I had found them on the ground. My five-year-old brain couldn't come up with anything better. "Well, what would you like to do with the treasure you found?" I started to pick nervously at my fingernails and asked through my teeth if she could take me to the store to buy some gum. "You're not allowed to chew gum. Put those in your piggy bank." I peered inside the hole where I dropped them through. They shone like diamonds in a sea full of pennies.

I still wanted that damned blueberry Hubba Bubba. I wanted to blow bubbles so big that the gum would pop and get stuck in my eyelashes. The next time I was at the store with my mother, I stuffed a pack in my pocket when she turned her back. My money was at home. I stole something and got away with it. I felt like a criminal but a happy one. I experienced my first thrill. I successfully shoplifted, and as we walked back to the car, I had a skip in my step and a smile on my face. I had gotten away with it.

When we got home from the Quik Check, I ran up the stairs to my room with my heart pounding inside my chest and tucked myself away in my closet behind three sizeable black garbage bags filled with clothes. There was a single light bulb with a long cotton string pull-chain in the ceiling directly above me, but I didn't bother reaching for it. I needed complete privacy. I grabbed the pack of blueberry Hubba Bubba out of my pocket and planned to chew the entire package up there, hidden in my closet. I unwrapped each piece and shoved them into my mouth. Just as the sugar started to release, I heard Mom calling me down for dinner. I quickly took the wad of sugary blueberry goodness out of my mouth and stuck it to the wall of the closet. Breathless and pumped with a cocktail of adrenaline and sugar, I showed up at the table for some meatloaf and potatoes. Nobody suspected a thing.

I had successfully stolen from a store, hidden what I had taken, and deceived my mom. At five years old, I had begun to learn the difference between right and wrong. The boy at Sunday school had done something wrong, and I knew that what I had done was wrong, but I couldn't help but feel just a little bit proud of myself. The tool of deception was now on my tool belt, and it would serve me well.

Seven

LYING WAS A HABIT, AND I WAS GOOD AT IT. I WATCHED my brother and his brand of lying, which wasn't at all very bright, because he was always getting caught. My father hated liars, and if he found out any of us were lying to him, we'd feel the effects for at least a week. Either we'd have trouble sitting for our meatloaf, or we'd be confined to our rooms until Mom took mercy on us and let us out.

Sometimes those bedrooms felt like cages. When sent to my room to think about what I did, I'd pass the time sitting in the front window on top of my toy chest and watch my neighborhood friends play outside. Every so often, I'd crack open the window and ask one of them to ring the doorbell to ask my mom if I could come out. A minute later, I'd see my friend walk a couple of steps backward into the grass to shake his head no.

I couldn't help but think Mom sent me up there because she didn't know what else to do with me. My brother and I continually tried her patience, and sometimes we'd push the wrong button and wind up in solitary. I'm sure there were other times when my mother just wanted a few quiet moments instead of having to deal with the constant bickering between my brother and me. She grasped at those moments of serenity whenever she could. Lord knows, in combination, my brother and I were much more work than two kids should have ever been. And there was also the question of my father. Who knew how he would be when he got home from work. Whether Mom had a valid reason for incarcerating us or not, I'm sure I wasn't up in my room for days like my mind imagined. I was probably in my room for maybe fifteen or twenty minutes at best. My mind has a fantastic ability to embellish and create different realities.

My room wasn't such a horrible place to be. It was a sanctuary where I could escape to other places and try on different versions of myself. It was a place where I could go to chew my packs of stolen gum in peace and breathe something other than the smoky haze of Carlton 100's downstairs in the kitchen. Most of my teenage years were spent up there, inside those peach and blue walls. It was either my room or sit around trying to ignore my brother, who was regularly tormenting Mom for no particular reason other than to amuse himself.

He'd start in with Mom with a smart-ass comment, and it set the ball rolling. Mom would react, and he would escalate. She made herself an easy target for his abuse. Once he started calling her names, she'd just sit there, staring at him with a blank expression on her face. Today, I recognize that behavior as hurt, but I didn't back then. I filed that in the folder labeled weakness. The one time she stood up for herself, my brother and I both wound up getting our asses beat. Dad did not react well to being called at work and asked to come home. What had started as an argument between Mom and my brother escalated when a knife appeared. I backed my brother up to the top of the stairs, gave a little push, and watched him tumble all the way to the bottom.

Dad worked only five minutes from the house. Mom's one panicked call had him there just as I was running out the front door. My brother and I were fucked. Dad yanked me by the arm and dragged me back into the house. He pushed past me and went right for my brother, picking him up by his neck and pinning him against the wall in the kitchen. "You wanna kill somebody? How about you start with me?" My father dropped him and walked away.

Eight

WHEN I WAS OLD ENOUGH TO UP AND LEAVE THE house with car keys, I stopped spending time at home. There was always arguing and yelling and then someone would start drinking, and things would go from bad to worse. It seemed like my brother was the reason for most of it. He was always in trouble. He was doing miserably in school, hanging out with the wrong kids, and had discovered the world of drugs and alcohol. Our family had begun to lose him before he had even shown up for life.

Who knows what was churning in his head, but if it resembled mine, there was probably a hamster high on cocaine bouncing around. If my brain didn't have an off switch, it was likely my brother didn't have one either. Everything is all or nothing, on or off, volcanic eruptions or eerie calm. The one thing that remained constant was chaos, and I did my best to stay away from that. I wasn't going to cower in fear behind a rocking chair, oh no. I was also done hiding in my room, and I refused to fight like my brother. I planned to get away. Run. And it kept me safe until it didn't.

While my brother was bleeding anger all over everyone his life touched, I was becoming a woman and found a new weapon to use. I wasn't the rejected flower girl anymore. I grew into that yellow dress and filled it out in all the right places. I knew early on what boys wanted, and now I was at the age that I could willingly give it to them.

I got called a lot of names when I was a kid, like *butter teeth*, because my teeth were discolored. *Horsehair* was a favorite because my hair was so long and unruly, T-Rex because my name wasn't a Jennifer, Kimberly, or Kelly, and most frequently *Spoiled Brat* because I didn't like it when my uncles or male cousins wanted hugs. I'd squirm, cry, and pitch a fit when any of them tried to get close. Worst of all was being called *Stupid*, and that came directly out of the mouth of my second-grade teacher. She told my parents at a parent-teacher conference that I'd never amount to being anything more than average. My favorite name, however, was *Slut*. That one gave me power.

In an attempt to stay out of the war zone that was our house, my brother and I would go hang out in the seventeenth-century cemetery just beyond the wide, black wrought iron gate in the rear of our yard. A short, worn gray-pebbled path sat below a reaching cluster of pine and oak trees that led to our sacred place. My brother and I would play here in all seasons, as the residents would never complain. In the winter, my brother and I would crouch behind the massive limestone rocks and throw snowballs at passing cars on the busy street just outside the fence. In the spring and summer, we played baseball, manhunt, and hide-and-seek with the neighborhood kids while we ignored the No Ball Playing sign the town posted.

We spent hours back there, my brother and I. A cemetery is a strange place to hang out, but old things and history fascinated me as a kid. I'd go back there alone just to look at the names and dates on the headstones and create stories about how these people lived their lives. Who were they, and what did they do in town? How did they die? Whatever their stories were, it was a quiet place to go. All the residents were long dead and didn't care that I was there, sitting six feet above them with my notebook and pen. It was in this cemetery behind my house that I first began to write. There was something about that place that was inspiring. It made me feel.

Being the weird girl who wrote alone in the cemetery didn't earn me very many friends in school. I was twelve, and I desperately wanted friends, but I was a freak, a weirdo. Writing in itself wasn't considered cool, and writing in a place of dead things was even less cool. I tried so hard to make friends, but it just didn't come. There was a mold to fill, and I was always overflowing, or not enough.

Nine

THE BUTTERED-TEETH, CEMETERY-DWELLING, BRAT-ty tomboy from Rose Place hung out somewhere in the in-between. I was a floater, a misfit, a reject. I wasn't able to identify with anyone around me in school. Nobody knew who I was any more than I did. Nobody couldn't slap a label on me as they did everyone else. I wasn't popular, a nerd, band geek, drama kid, athlete, burnout, cool Asian kid, or cheerleader. I wasn't in choir, boosters, keys, or honors, but I was a girl who was desperate to fit in somewhere. I just couldn't.

I didn't mind being alone, for the most part. Alone in my own company was safe. There was nobody to yell at me, stir up drama, call me names, or treat me like a soldier on the alcoholic battle-ground that had become my homelife. Yet, I still needed people. I needed them in an all-encompassing, terrifying, paralyzing way.

I was always an observant kind of kid growing up. I watched how people acted, listened to what they said and didn't say. I read body language and was able to sense things in other people like anxiety, nervousness, and anger. It was kind of my thing to predict behavior, and by the time I was a teenager, I had gotten very good at it. I figured that I could use this talent to make some friends and, eventually, I did make a couple of them. They didn't hang out in graveyards for fun, but they were different, too, just like me.

There was my friend Louise, with the frayed orange hair, burnt and thin from using too much Sun-In over the summer. There was Jen, a long, lean girl with pretty green eyes. And finally there was Nicole, but I called her "Nikki," a full-blooded and full-bodied Italian girl whose parents owned the local storage place. Late at night, we'd sneak into the office and make copies of our boobs for fun. Our group of misfits was inseparable. We moved about Theodore Schor Middle as a single unit, making us less of a target. Going at it alone meant taking the risk of gum being stuck in our hair, losing our armful of books as someone ran by purposely knocking them out of our hands, and being picked on relentlessly for the things that made us different.

We didn't mind being the girls we were, but it bothered everyone else around us. We still got teased and picked on. We were still the losers that got their school clothes thrown into the toilet during gym class and ridiculed to no end for the way we looked and acted. We spent our days being our awkward selves, and it made other kids uncomfortable and angry. And where was God? Why wasn't He on my side? If the God I had learned about in Sunday school didn't protect me at home or school, I had absolutely no proof He existed at all. I just wanted to fit in, to be accepted, to be loved, and if God didn't protect or love me, I was going to set my sail in the direction of someone who did.

Ten

BOY CRAZY IS WHAT MY LITTLE GROUP OF MISFITS
were, but boys took very little interest in us. None of us was anything spectacular to look at and we all knew it. Boys wanted nothing
to do with girls like us. I started digging into my mother's make-up
bag, hoping to find a cure for my ugliness. I was determined to
stand out, make myself a swan among my friends.

I had no idea how to put make-up on my face. I used to watch
my mom paint her face in the passenger seat mirror from the back
seat of the Datsun. It was a wonder to me how she applied mascara
in a moving vehicle, because I was standing completely still and
poking my eyes with the brush. I found her *ravishing red* lipstick,
hoping that I could stop traffic by smattering it across my thin lips.
Power and attention are what I wanted, and *ravishing red* was my
ticket to the top.

I had spackled one too many layers of paint on my face, and the
kids at school found yet another reason to make fun of me. Only

Ms. Schmidt, my first-period language arts teacher, took hold of my face in her hands and told me that I looked beautiful. I asked to go to the bathroom, and I washed my mask right off my face. What Ms. Schmidt told me wasn't worth a damn. I wanted the admiration and attention of boys. I wanted them to find me beautiful. I wanted someone to desire me, and I soon found out what worked.

Naturally, my parents and friends didn't approve of what I decided I would be wearing from now on. I, too, realized my choices of outfits were questionable, but I wanted what I wanted and was willing to go to any length to get it. On my grandma's buck, I traded in my bland button-down blouses, frumpy jeans, and worn-out Keds for a black leather-fringed jacket, black miniskirts, black stockings, and black leather-fringed ankle boots. My brand new persona was complete with an attitude overhaul. I was a self-proclaimed cool kid now, and people took notice.

The coolest kids were drinkers and smokers. They skipped class for cigarette breaks in bathrooms and hung out backstage in the auditorium, where teachers would never think to look for them, and behind the school by the cafeteria dumpster. I was attracted to the older boys with their flannel shirts, hair down to their shoulders, torn Levis, and biker boots. Plumes of smoke and sex rose above them, creating for this young and impressionable teen an atmosphere of mystery and intrigue. The worse the boy behaved, the better.

Of course, this sudden change in me didn't take right away. This genius attention-seeking plan of mine was received by a whole lot of *what the fuck do you think you're doing* questions. Nikki, especially, was not a fan of my transformation. "Everyone around is going to think you're a slut. Look at you. What is wrong with you?" I refused to even look at Nikki for weeks. Is that what she thinks of me? Am I a slut? Well, to hell with her and good riddance. I didn't need her anyway. No love lost.

She moved to some sunny beach in Florida that summer, and I never heard from her again, but I took her comment personally. If she thought I was a slut, then a lot of other people probably thought so too. I decided that day that I'd do whatever I wanted, whenever I wanted, and with whomever I wanted. If I were a slut, then I'd show her what a slut truly is. What backward, fucked-up thinking that was, but that was my brain—zero to a hundred in one sentence.

I marched my eighth-grade black-clad spiteful ass right out to that smoker's pit right the first day back at school and told the coolest looking kid to give me a cigarette. If he did, I promised to meet him in the cemetery behind my house after school. I had no intention of smoking that cigarette, but I knew it was my way into the crowd. Mike lit my Camel for me and handed it over. I took one drag, choked for a good five minutes, and stomped it out on the ground. Smoking wasn't for me, but Mike sure was, and he was looking at me like I was a vanilla ice cream cone. I slipped my phone number into the front pocket of his red flannel shirt and told him to call me after school.

Two minutes after I walked in the door, Mike called. He was on his way to the cemetery to make good on our trade. I panicked. "Please don't let anyone see you, especially my mom." She and my father were keeping a close eye on me since my transformation months before. So far, they had convinced themselves it was just a phase I was going through and would someday snap out of it just as quickly as I had stepped into it, but it was no phase.

I showed Mike the large headstone my brother and I used to hide behind to throw snowballs at unsuspecting cars on Stelton Road. I laid down in the tall grass behind the stone and let him lay on top of me. He began to touch me over my clothes, squeezing my breasts. I felt something in me come alive. It felt good. I met Mike there in that cemetery for weeks, but over the clothes was as far as anything went. As much as he tried for more, my answer was always no. Mike didn't like the fact that I wouldn't allow him to go any further with me and told everyone by the cafeteria dumpster that I was a slut. They believed him, and so did I. If I let this boy touch me as I did, then how could I not be? I was never more grateful for the school year to end. My entire eighth-grade year was nothing more than torture and name-calling, and I realized that it was all my fault. It was the beginning of the end for me or the start of a slow downward spiral into oblivion.

Eleven

MY LOVE AFFAIR WITH ALCOHOL BEGAN WHEN I WAS fourteen years old, and for me, it was love at first sip. My brain lit up like Christmas morning as I felt the warmth of the liquid travel down my throat and into my stomach, where it danced around like fireflies in a jar. Almost instantly my guard fell away, and I thought this is what it must be like to feel good. No wonder so many adults around me drank. Who wouldn't if the result felt like freedom?

My parents used to take my brother and me to parties all the time, because parties meant free and endlessly flowing alcohol until the kegs ran dry, and someone was making horrible decisions they wouldn't remember. At one of these parties, my brother and I found a barrel full of ice-cold kiwi-strawberry wine coolers. Nobody had been paying attention to us and, as long as the pitcher was still pouring beer, nobody would. My brother and I were left to our devices at these things anyway. People came to parties to drink as much as they could, or so it seemed. After a couple of hours, it was as if my brother and I had disappeared altogether in a thick fog of Marlboro smoke and Budweiser.

My brother dug his hand deep down into the ice and fished out a Bartles & Jaymes, popped the top, and handed it to me. "You first," he said. I liked the beachy picture on the front of the bottle. It looked like such a relaxing paradise with its palm trees and turquoise-blue ocean with giant pieces of juicy-looking fruit dangling above it. I brought the bottle up to my nose and smelled the sweet scent of strawberries. "Well, go ahead and drink it already, you chicken. It's not a fistful of quarters," my brother said. I glanced around one more time to make sure nobody was looking and then chugged the entire bottle. Immediately I felt light, dizzy, warm, and euphoric right down to my toes. My brother and I bonded that day with our new friends, Bartles & Jaymes.

We talked about how much we hated our lives, how bad our teachers sucked, how much people sucked, and how much we hated coming to these dumb parties with our parents all the time. Then, a switch flipped inside my brother, and he became angry. Something in his head was moving at rapid-fire, and there was no stopping it. He stood up, kicked over the barrel, and ran off somewhere. My brother was a fighter. He fought everything and everyone. At first, it was a challenge for him to see just how far he could push people before they would react. He wanted to piss people off. He wanted attention and approval just as severely as I did. Only he had a different method: anger and frustration.

But my brother's story is not mine to tell. He has his particular brand of pain and suffering that is unique to him. I can sit here and wish to the very end of my life that he finds the courage to unmask it and use that pain for good, but all the wishes in the world won't save someone from themselves. Some fighters never leave the ring.

Twelve

MY NEWLY FOUND *FRIENDS*, BARTLES & JAYMES, AND I started high school together. With the courage they gave me, I was no longer anxious or shy. There were a lot more different kinds of kids at the high school, and I got along with a whole bunch of them, spanning across all the known cliques. With a class of nearly seven hundred kids, I fit in just fine and was able to easily blend into the background, fly under the radar, and keep my head down low. I knew where to find trouble and what I needed to do to get in it, so I figured if nobody could see me, then nobody would know what I'm doing. Nobody would ever know.

The way I looked didn't exactly go over well with the girls; some of them were downright nasty. And the easy way I had with being a smart-ass, witty, and funny with the guys irritated the crap out of them because guys love that. They flocked to me like moths to a flame. Every other guy I met said, "There's something about you that's different, but I'm not sure what." I'm not like other girls.

I sought out the loners, the news kids, the ones who didn't talk much, and the ones blending in just like me. They were there, existing in space, floating in their antigravity, not attracting nor repelling anything around them, except for me. A freak can pick out another freak easily. My closest friend was *newly American*, having emigrated from South Korea a year before. She spoke broken English, but I understood Jennie, and she understood me. We were both outsiders, square picture frames holding together colorful landscapes that went ignored.

I met Amelia in an English class. Her mom was an alcoholic that never wanted her, and her dad was just along for the ride. Amelia was a mistake, and she went about her life thinking that she was on this earth strictly by accident. She was a resentment, just a tiny little blip on the radar her mom kept trying to scrape off. Amelia wrote poetry, loved music, and was horrible at tennis. She was a tomboy like me, but absolutely no part of her was interested in being a girl at all.

Those were my two friends, my two best friends, my only friends. Others were just passing by or easily forgettable, and some I just wanted to steer clear. Again, I was a floater not being able to identify with any particular group. I tried to tell myself that I was confident, strong-willed, and independent and didn't care what anyone thought about me, but that was a lie. I figured if I lied to myself enough and held on tight, I would survive just fine. I knew that even if most of the girls at school didn't like me, the boys did. At least I always had the boys.

And I did meet a boy, Antonio. He had bright-green eyes, silky olive skin, and thick black hair and volunteered his time with the town's rescue squad and hung with fellow wannabe first responders, officers, and firefighters.

Antonio, oh, how I wanted Antonio, and getting my hands on him was easier than I thought. I smiled at him over a bowl of noodles in the cafeteria, and he smiled back. Jennie took her nose out of her Seventeen magazine. "What the fuck you doing? Don't you know about that guy? He's two years older than you. Trouble," she said. I loved the sound of that word, trouble. Trouble meant pushing the limits, teetering on the edge of disaster, almost jumping off the cliff but not quite. Trouble meant dipping your toes in the water just enough so there's no splash.

One smile from across the cafeteria, and he asked me out. I fought hard to push down my excitement and play it cool as I said yes, but I was a giddy little school girl all over again with a crush and a dream of falling in love. There was only one thing standing in the way of our love: my parents. They'd never approve of me dating an older boy. They didn't approve of me dating at all.

It turns out I didn't mind going to those parties with my parents anymore once I found out that Antonio went to them too. Now the town of Piscataway, my parents, brother, Antonio, and I happily celebrated the baptisms of fire engines. Every week I'd ask my parents if there were any wet downs nearby because I knew he'd be there. My parents, still drawn by the lure of kegs filled with Budweiser, never raised an eyebrow with my sudden interest in going to these once-aggravating events. I'd be able to see Antonio, and my parents couldn't say no. It was the perfect opportunity to be sneaky but not too sneaky.

After grabbing a couple of Bartles & Jaymes from the always-available and unattended barrel, Antonio and I would meet up in the woods to be alone. There, I'd let him do things, although I was never really an active participant in any of it. Physically I was there, but mentally I was checked out. It was that way for me all the time now. I needed that wine to relax, and when I did, I just went somewhere else. I felt no emotion, connection, or excitement. I saw myself up against a tree being felt up by this guy as if I was watching from an upper branch. He was touching me, kissing me, and rubbing his erection against my pelvis, but I felt nothing. I just wanted him to like me, and I didn't care what it took.

The woods weren't enough. He was demanding more of me and more frequently. To keep my romance hidden from my parents, I began sneaking off after school, telling my mom that I was going to Jennie's house to study. Jennie would cover for me, and my unsuspecting mother had no reason to check up on me. I'd meet Antonio everywhere and anywhere. No area of town was off-limits to us. Parks, tennis courts, schoolyards, abandoned buildings, his friend's houses, cars, and even his little sister's pink playhouse were all perfect places for us to hide. Not only was Antonio getting what he wanted from me, which was nearly everything, I noticed that he was also becoming increasingly aggressive toward me each time we'd meet.

He'd kiss a little too hard, push and shove me a little bit, and squeeze my breasts so hard they hurt, but I convinced myself that it was his passion for me. He loved me so much that he just couldn't control what he was doing, and I kept letting him as I held my breath to keep from screaming. I knew it was only a matter of time before he wanted more than what I wanted to give. I was fourteen.

A couple of years ago, I had still been playing with Barbies, but by looking at everyone around me at school, there was one thing in common with all twelve hundred of us: hormones. I didn't seem to have them yet, but everyone else around me was emanating sex. It hung in the air like clouds discharging lightning. It felt like I was standing in the middle of it, holding a metal rod straight up above me, screaming, "Strike me! Strike me! I want to come alive." I just wanted to be like everyone else.

And because of it, I became willing to give Antonio what he wanted. After school, on a Wednesday in November 1990, I hopped on my ten-speed and peddled my way across town to Antonio's house, feeling like my lunch was going to wind up on the sidewalk. He was there, waiting on his front porch, arms crossed, with a tightly perched smirk on his face, which I didn't understand. I followed him inside and into his bedroom on the second floor. All I saw was a bed and a condom on it. There may have been other furniture and things there, too, but I couldn't see any of it. There was tunnel vision or some sort of short movie clip on loop that prevented me from seeing anything but the condom on the bed. My heart started pounding in my chest, and sweat was beading up and dripping down my back. My face grew hot and red. I could feel it and kept touching my face.

"I can't. I just can't do this. I thought that I could. I told you I wanted to and all, and I do, but I don't know now. I don't think I can. I, I just can't." I was rambling. I could even hear myself sounding stupid. But it was too late. I rejected him after I had promised him that I'd give him what I didn't have.

I grabbed my backpack and ran out the front door to find my mother sitting outside in her van. "Get your ass home right now!"

Fuck. I'm going to get killed.

My mother is going to chain me to the walls of my room. My father would bolt my door shut and feed me bread under the door. My ass is grass, as my dad would say.

I was just about a block away from getting my ass home when a girl who I knew from school jumped out of a bush and sucker punched me right in the face. I stopped. What the hell?

"I run the fucking school, bitch! Not you."

Umm, ok. "I don't understand. What are you talking about?"

She was fired up. "Someone told me you think you're popular, and I'm here to tell you you're not."

What? Where did she hear that crap? "I'm sorry. I don't even really know who you are. What's the problem?"

She hit me again. I got back on my bike and took off.

When I walked into the house, my mother was standing right there, right in front of me with her arms crossed and eyes glaring. "Wait a minute…" She looked at me. "What happened to your face?"

I took a deep breath and closed my eyes. Maybe she's distracted by this now. "Some crazy girl punched me. Twice!" I cried.

My mother grabbed her car keys off the kitchen table, blew past me, and sped off in the direction in which I came. I stood there paralyzed, not knowing what to think or what to do. What lies can I come up with to cover my ass? I asked myself.

My brother came in then, mid-daydream. "Hey, I heard you got your ass beat."

How the hell would he know? I had just gotten home less than five minutes ago. My brother smiled. That fucker had set me up.

Thirteen

THINGS IN MY LIFE THEN SEEMED TO BE GOING FROM bad to worse. Not only had I freaked out on Antonio, gotten sucker punched, and been grounded for four months, but poor, rejected Antonio went back to school the next day and bragged to his friends that he had sex with me. The lie spread like wildfire. Even the teachers were looking at me sideways. I went right back to being that slut again.

Of course she slept with him; just look at her.

And for some ungodly reason, Antonio still expected me to be his girlfriend because he was just that wonderful of a guy. Antonio was lying, but it was my word against his, so when I tried to explain myself, people just laughed.

If you had sex with him, you don't gotta lie about it.

The next morning, I saw him leaning up against the wall near my homeroom, flipping a toothpick around in his mouth with that same stupid smirk on his face I had seen a couple of days before. I wanted to smack it off his stupid face for ruining my life. He snapped his fingers and pointed down to the ground next to him, signaling me to come over to him like a dog that was to obey its master. Fuck that. I walked right past him. I learned by the end of homeroom that he was sending the same girl who sucker punched me to finish the job. Not only had Antonio been rejected, but being disrespected in front of his friends was worse. I couldn't understand why all of this crap was happening to me. I was a slut with a whole host of enemies at school now. People hated me, whispered behind my back, laughed when I walked by, and rolled their eyes. I hid in the senior bathroom and cried. I thought about calling home to ask my mom if she would come to pick me up, but I knew she wouldn't, so I just sat there on the floor of the last stall, crying my way through a roll of toilet paper. That girl never did come after me, but I took a kitchen knife to school with me for weeks afterward. If someone were to jump me, they'd get a steak knife to the gut. I minded my own business, kept to myself, and never spoke badly of anyone. And I was still this large target for everyone, a plaything, a toy. I was used, lied on, and disregarded. The only person who seemed to care or wanted to listen was Grandma, so I picked up the phone and cried in her ear for over an hour.

She was my protector, lead-footed in her red Buick Skylark, with a two-inch gold cross around her neck to slay any monsters that came close to her or her darling favorite grandbaby. She knew that it was hard for me at school, she told me what to do about Antonio, and she knew what my life was like at home. My mom had started drinking now to cope with my brother's ever-escalating lousy behavior and my father's wrath. I couldn't blame her. If I had her life, I'd be drinking myself to death, I thought. By the time I was eighteen, I had come up with several scenarios in which to make my grand escape from the increasing emotional, verbal, and physical violence at home. I would leave. Cut! End scene! But I didn't because Grandma was there and often saved me.

We wrote letters and called each other every week. I'd spend summers with her at the lake, eating banana Yoplait and powdered doughnuts. She gave me a book about birds and challenged me to find and name each different bird that I saw. I stared out her back bedroom window for hours, watching birds and listening to the wind whooshing through the pine trees, taking in the calm and gentle moments of serenity.

Grandma let me bang out tunes on her Wurlitzer as she tried to sing a made-up song to whatever melody I played. I rode with Grandpa in his little tan diesel fuel Volkswagen Rabbit, helping him do odd jobs around the retirement community he and Grandma lived in. I happily accepted payment in jellybeans and Starlight Mints. We went bowling and fishing and enjoyed holiday and birthday dinners gathered around Grandma's Ethan Allen turn-of-the-century dining room table. They said grace with heads bowed, giving thanks to Lord Jesus for our food and our family.

Grandma and Grandpa were love, warmth, and safety. They were trust and security, happy, joyous, and full of God. They let me be the kid I was supposed to be. Grandma and Grandpa's house was my remote island far away from the land of everything and nothing. It felt good not to have to live inside of my head for a little while. My head was turning out to be the worst place to be. It was starting to get crowded up there with so many voices telling me who I was, and ultimately I'd listen to all the wrong ones. They were the loudest.

I hated to go back home after my visits with Grandma because it meant going back to reality. Grandma's house was just a vacation, just pretend, a fairy-tale snippet of what it's like to have my soul loved. I sat in the backseat of my mom's mint-green Cadillac, staring out the window, hands and forehead smashed up against the glass. Grandma would stand on her front porch and blow me kisses goodbye, and I would sniffle and cry half the way home.

Fourteen

MY BROTHER AND I BEGAN TO REBEL IN THE JEKYLL-and-Hyde atmosphere that was our home. When the scotch came out, we scattered like dropped toothpicks. It did horrible things to my father, who was otherwise caring and reserved. It turned him into an unpredictable, angry monster. He would be happy and harmonious with the first couple of drinks, but then, as he kept going, something changed in him. He lost control.

Sometimes I'd make the mistake of going into the kitchen as the sound of ice cubes went clunking into an empty glass, unaware of how many drinks had already been consumed. Sometimes I was caught sneaking my way to the refrigerator and had to accept an invitation for a *talk*. One of his talks, I always knew, was only ever a lecture about life and how hard it was going to be for me *in the real world*. I had no concept of the real world, and I wouldn't until I was a functioning part of it, but rather than poke the bear, I knew to keep my mouth shut. I nodded and grunted until he told me I could leave.

Even if I could respond to him, I never did. I was too scared to look at him the wrong way, no less say anything. Sometimes even the wrong look was seen as being disrespectful. My brother would poke his head out the door with his imaginary gun pointed at Dad and ready to fire. He wouldn't even put a toe out to test the waters; he was ablaze and prepared to burn down the whole place if he had to. A lecture over scotch would often turn into my brother's ass-whooping. He'd ask something as inconsequential as, "What's going on out there?" And my dad would go from zero to a hundred proof in less than thirty seconds. My brother knew very well what was going on, and maybe he poked the bear to get him away from me. Whatever his intentions, Dad would eventually mellow, and good times would be back again.

I reflect fondly on those happy times. The Saturday afternoons when Mom was singing and dancing to Bruce Springsteen spinning on the turntable and Dad was out back grilling up London broil for dinner had everyone in a good mood. My brothers and I had an overwhelming sense of ease during these times, as it seemed they were few and far between. My parents were busy raising us and gave little time to their own lives.

Maybe they drank to unwind, to deal with the stress of it all. It's not the healthiest way to handle life's struggles, but I understand it. My parents bent over backward to give my brother and me ample opportunity to explore and grow in our interests. They threw the ball into our court and left us with the job of finding our rackets, a place to hang our hats.

Mom trudged me off to dance class four days a week, doing my hair buns and make-up more times than I can count, shuttling me all over the tristate area for dance competitions and endless performances. Dad took me to Brownie meetings and dedicated himself to a father-daughter activity called Indian Princesses. Neither of my parents ever missed a ball game, dance recital, or school function.

They were ever-present in my life. Dad soothed my broken hearts, holding me while I cried for hours in his arms, and he'd cry, too, wishing to take my pain away. When I became a woman at the tender age of eleven, Dad came home from work with a dozen roses. Later, he'd walk me down the aisle and give me away, only to continue to help my husband and me buy our first home. He was good like that.

The funniest thing about him was the things he said. Excuses are for losers, suck it up, and Nike's tagline, just do it, were among my favorites. Any time I didn't feel like doing something or complained about how shitty things were going, Dad was always answering my aches and pains with one of those stellar comebacks. I didn't care much for them at the time, but I find my dad coming out of my mouth with my kids because, no, life isn't that bad. Everything is temporary, even life itself. He taught me to put on my big-girl britches and carry on with a brave face.

Fifteen

I DIDN'T DRINK MUCH AS A TEENAGER. ASIDE FROM A handful of stolen wine coolers and a sip here and there from my mother's wine glass when she wasn't looking, I wasn't interested in liquor. I was observing what alcohol was doing to my family members, and that was enough for me to try and stay a safe distance away. I knew liquor did nothing for me except make me sick, give me headaches, turn my father into a person I was afraid of, make my mother cry, and send my brother to prison.

But I was still trying to fit in at that stupid high school of mine. I had done everything from failing classes on purpose to blowing off Saturday detentions for skipping class. I walked around armed and dangerous, choked on cigarettes while hidden in bathroom stalls with the cool girls, and flirted with boys no matter if I liked them or not. Mostly, I hadn't studied for tests, and being *friendly* was a great way for me to cheat off their papers, copy their homework, and bum pieces of gum.

Sadly, I was still just looking for approval, attention, and a sense of belonging somewhere, anywhere. I thought that maybe I'd find it in the tight end of the high school football team, although he quickly dropped me for a younger, more popular model. Who am I kidding anyway? Tommy was beautiful, and so were all of his friends. They were talented athletes, all with eyes looking toward dreams more significant than themselves. I was just me, nothing special.

I had short-lived fame with Tommy. I was the envy of every girl around me. Whenever I walked down the school's hallways hand in hand with him, heads turned and people whispered behind cupped hands. And had horses been allowed to hitch up at the school, they would have bowed. I felt like royalty, like I was beautiful and meant something to someone. As brief as it was, I felt alive. I had finally arrived at my destination. I had gotten my foot in the door with the cool kids crowd. The pinnacle of my high school career, senior year, was an invitation to a New Year's Eve party at a local hotel.

Someone's older sister had rented a room, supplied liquor and drugs, and let all of us underage kids run amuck. I wanted to go. I wanted to be with all the cool kids, but I also knew my father would never let me go to a party. It was hard enough for me to go to the movies with a guy, no less a big party. I thought for days about how I'd ask and what lies I could muster up and gathered possible alibis. Luckily, my brother became a distraction of the highest magnitude, and my parents temporarily forgot I was even around. While my parents were busy tearing my brother a new asshole for what he had done, I weaseled my way over to my mother and dropped the question as quickly as possible. "Hey, my friend is having a New Year's Eve party tomorrow night. Can I go?" My mother, in her rage, looked past me and nodded her head. I quickly packed a bag, got in my car, and took off for Motel 6, room 201.

Room 201 was full of kids with whom I didn't normally associate. A tall, lanky-looking blond guy I had never seen before handed me a red Solo cup and told me the keg was in the bathtub. "Don't spill. Party foul!" Whatever that meant. I worked my way past two couples, hands and mouths occupied, to the bathroom. And there in the tub was the giant silver keg, right in the middle of the bathtub, just as the lanky guy had said. The problem was, I didn't know how to get the beer out, so rather than look like a total dumbass, asking someone how to get a drink out of this thing, I tossed my cup into the trash and went in search of something a little less complicated. Tommy was sitting on the edge of a stain-soaked 1970s-style comforter that was on the floor, holding a drink in his hand, ready to party.

"This is for you, cupcake. I had my sister pick it up for us." He handed me a bottle of fruit punch Mad Dog 20/20, a popular drink of underage, middle-class, suburban white kids everywhere. I sat down next to Tommy and some girl who was gulping cheap vodka straight from the bottle. I grabbed the bottle of Mad Dog and drank the entire thing inside a half an hour. "Girl, you are fucking crazy! I love it," Tommy wailed. I had no idea why he was so animated. I felt perfectly fine until the room started to spin. I was going to throw up.

I ran for the bathroom only to find the vodka-chugging chick passed out with her head on the rim of the toilet. I pulled her off the bowl by her hair and told her I was going to be sick. She said, "Fuck you, bitch! Leave me the fuck alone. Don't you see I'm dying here? Find another toilet." I stumbled out of the bathroom crashing into the walls, sat down on one of the beds, and threw up all over the floor. Needless to say, if I had earned any *cool* points by being at that party, they were all gone now, and I'd be back to the same old nobody soon enough.

I still don't remember how I got home that night, or even if it was the next day, but I woke up in my bed at home, drenched in sweat, head pounding, car keys in hand. I came out of my bedroom to see my father standing there, just outside my door. "Good morning. Rough night?"

I brushed past him and toward the bathroom. "Not now, Dad. I'm going to be sick." And I was, all day long. I guess my intolerable hangover was punishment enough because neither one of my parents ever said a word about it. I swore up and down to God above and the devil below that I'd never drink again.

Sixteen

THE DOORS TO HIGH SCHOOL FINALLY CLOSED. I HAD made it out alive. While the rest of my class was weeping through goodbyes, I took off without even making eye contact with anyone. Peace! I'm out. See you dumb fucks never. After prom weekend went sour a few weeks before, I was done with the bullshit.

I went to senior prom with Tommy, Jennie, and Jennie's boyfriend from New York, whom I doubted had even existed until the day he showed up at my house for the limo ride to prom. I knew just by looking at this kid that he was not the twenty-one-year-old Jennie led me to believe. He wasn't a day over sixteen, at best, and now he was riding in our limousine to the Sheraton.

I was looking forward to prom as much as the weekend away at the Jersey shore that would follow. Kids from my class had hotel and motel rooms booked months in advance. Dad had only told me the night before prom that, yes, I could go. Since I was going with a small group and not just Tommy, it would be all right. Dad gave me twenty bucks and told me to have a good time.

Prom was lackluster, the drive down the shore was a treat, and trying to find a motel room when we got there wasn't easy. Not one single place had a vacancy. It was Memorial Day weekend, the biggest weekend for shore-goers everywhere. I'm sure my dad knew this and had hoped that I would just turn around and come back home, but I was eighteen and stubborn as all get up. We'd find somebody who would let us shack up with them. I didn't care if I had to sleep on a balcony. I was determined to prove that I was a grown-up, totally capable of being on my own for a weekend. My parents hadn't allowed me to do much as a teenager. It was as if I was forbidden to have fun, and now that I had a little bit of freedom to have a good time, I was dead set on making that happen. We'd figure out all the details when we got there.

Tommy threw two cases of Coronas in the trunk of his '88 Monte Carlo, and the four of us were off to Wildwood for the weekend. No air conditioning in his car meant we had all the windows rolled down, with the sweet sounds of L. L. Cool J and KRS-One announcing us as we tore down the Garden State Parkway. The four of us were a crew, young adults with no sense of responsibility or a care in the world. We were on our own.

We got about halfway there when the good old '88 Monte Carlo broke down. Tommy told all of us not to worry about it, that we'd just get a tow into town. We gathered all our money together and got towed to a Getty station somewhere in Wildwood. Jennie wanted to call her parents to come get her, but I told her not to. Calling her parents would be admitting defeat, and we weren't going to let a little car trouble ruin our weekend. We left the car behind and headed six blocks down to the boardwalk.

We scoured that boardwalk for hours looking for friends. I knew none of mine were there, since my only other friend was Amelia, and she wasn't allowed to go. Instead, she had to spend her weekend serving ice cream at the Greenbrook Friendly's. Jennie's friends were an enigma of their own, taking off for a weekend in the city instead of the beach. All that remained at the shore that weekend was the mass of Tommy's beautiful friends. The ones who didn't like me because I was a sloppy drunk who couldn't hold her liquor. We did eventually run into some of Tommy's friends who were all thrilled to see him by the high fives and bro hugs he was getting. They completely ignored me as if I wasn't even standing there next to him at all. Tommy stuck his hands in his pockets and looked at the ground mumbling something to a friend about letting us stay with them.

His friend looked over at me and said, "Not if she's with you."

"That's fucked up. She's my girl."

"Well, I don't care if she's Julia Roberts. That white trash ain't staying in my room." It was the same story as everyone else. Nobody would let us stay as long as I was with him. We had decided it was just another minor detail, and everything would work out.

We spent our day relaxing on the beach with nothing but our swimsuits and towels. None of us geniuses had thought to bring as much as a bottle of water with us. It was hot as hell, and we were dehydrating, but we were dehydrating on a beach in Wildwood, so we called it good. Then night rolled around, and we were all now thirsty, hungry, and homeless. Nobody wanted us. Nobody wanted me. We had spent Tommy's last few dollars on sunscreen, pizza, and four cokes. Again, Jennie sat there dark-faced in the diner, wanting to call her parents, and again I told her no.

She screamed at me. "Are you fucking insane? We have to sleep outside tonight like the homeless." Still, I did not care. None of us were calling our parents for rescue. We'd worry about things tomorrow. The four of us slept huddled together under the board-walk, near the sign that said, "Beach Closes at Dusk, Trespassers Will Be Prosecuted to the Full Extent of the Law."

Tomorrow wound up being a repeat of the day before, only now we were hanging out in the diners, ordering hot water with lemon because we were out of money. Then, one of us remembered we had beer in the trunk of Tommy's car that was currently still sitting at the Getty station, waiting for repairs. We walked the six blocks back to the gas station to claim our prize. The cases of Corona had spent two days in the trunk at about ninety-five degrees.

"Hot beer, anyone?" I looked at Tommy like he had three heads. "Aww, come on, this is liquid gold," he said.

"Yeah, liquid gold, all right. Hot gold piss!" I groaned.

He popped the top off the first one and chugged it down right there in the Getty gas station parking lot. Just then, a mechanic came out of the office and told us it would be $1200 to fix the car. Tommy chugged another beer, then another. Between the four of us defeated souls, we managed to drink both cases of hot piss in the parking lot in a matter of a couple of hours. Tommy called his sister, and she wired us the money. Seventeen hours and four pounding headaches later, we were home.

"Did you have a good weekend?"

"Yeah, Dad. We had a great time. Lots of fun." And that was the end of that. So after graduation, I couldn't be happier knowing that I never had to see any of those assholes again, Tommy included. Now, how the hell do I get out of my parents' house?

Seventeen

MY BROTHER WAS BECOMING EVEN MORE SELF-DE-structive. At nineteen, he was drinking a lot more now and wound up on life support after wrapping his car around a telephone pole on the way home from a party. It was evident to me that he had a problem, but from my point of view, it seemed my parents were turning somewhat of a blind eye to it. Maybe admitting that my brother had an issue would make them have to question their behavior. I can't speculate, but everything wasn't *hunky-dory*, as my dad liked to say about how life was going.

In reality, things were falling apart. That's what happens when you pretend that everything is fine. Maybe if you ignore a problem, it will either disappear or fix itself in time. Perhaps if you don't acknowledge a problem, it simply didn't exist. "God's got a plan for your brother," my grandmother always said. As the nurse began to pull him out of his coma, he grabbed ahold of my hand and wouldn't let go. His eyes had desperation in them, as if he was pleading for help that nobody could give. I believed my grandma. But God? I didn't want anything to do with that guy.

I was angry. I had been furious. God had never been anywhere I was. He didn't protect, shield, or heal me of anything. He let that boy touch and abuse me in Sunday school. Everyone I had trusted and loved had failed me, and my brother was angry and suffering right along with me. Where was God in our lives? Where was this loving character in the sky, watching over us? My God wasn't loving. He was vengeful, hateful, and punishing. Grandma also used to tell me that God would never give me more than I could handle. I had no idea how much He would give.

Eighteen

MY ESCAPE WOULD BE COLLEGE, BUT MY GRADES
and sad SAT scores had me going to the county school known by all
as the thirteenth and fourteenth grades. I wasn't smart enough to
get into a real college. I had spent all of my high school years trying
to fit in, not thinking about my future.

I did struggle in school, especially early. I was significantly behind in both reading and math and had special classes to help me
catch up with my peers, but the math stuff never stuck. My brain
just didn't work that way. I had a couple of people along the way
telling me that I was a gifted writer, but I never believed them. I was
pegged as stupid early on, and one *stupid* outweighed four *talented*
any day of the week.

My love of writing began at the age of eight. I was in the second
grade and excited each morning to come into the classroom and
read the writing prompt on the chalkboard. Each day, there would

be a new one: write five sentences about a cat; write five sentences on what you want to be when you grow up; write five sentences about your favorite vacation. I couldn't wait to grab my pencil and take it to that fresh sheet of white lined paper. I could write anything my mind could dream. The best days were the days when the chalkboard said Free Write, which meant I could write about anything I wanted. I wrote poetry.

Even at eight years old, I found poetry to be a fulfilling and meaningful way to express myself. I could be as creative with words as I wanted. Poetry always felt like I was weaving a tapestry of emotion. My insides spilled out from heart to paper, leaving behind a pencil and paper trail of black and white, loud and in color. Poetry was and is my most authentic self and the most natural medium to share my feelings. A piece of writing can be dissected a thousand times and interpreted in a thousand different ways, but only the writer truly knows what those words mean.

Whole stories unfold within just one poem. On one of the exciting *free write* days, I sat down at my desk and picked up my pencil, and this flowed from my little eight-year-old heart:

I wanted to hide.
My special place.
It's a large house with seventeen bedrooms.
I'll take just one bed in one room
and go under it.
I'll bring a pillow, so my head can lay soft.
I'll bring my dolls to play with.

Sometimes I might peek out from underneath.
Someday, someone will want to share,
and I will let them.
For now, it's my special place.

I got a *C* on that piece of writing. It was something I was proud to have written. My face beamed as I turned it into my teacher. I had taken pride in my work, and my pride earned me a *C*. She didn't believe that I wrote it. I couldn't have. No eight-year-old can write like that. But I could. I look at that same piece of writing today in my folder titled Old Poems, and I know that poem is anything but average. I continued to write because writing made me happy. It makes me feel alive and releases all my pain.

Nineteen

IN THE THIRTEENTH AND FOURTEENTH GRADES, I still had my two solids, Amelia and Jennie, but Jennie went off to a real college, and Amelia went to work for Friendly's full-time. I was on my own at the junior college and fully committed to taking my education seriously for a change. One thing was missing, though, a boyfriend, and that had to change.

I didn't care much about making friends because I found people to be disappointing. I did a fantastic job keeping to myself and minding my own business. It was easier to blend in with a few thousand faces of strangers. I would find myself trying my best not to stand out, even glaring at people who even attempted to start a conversation with me. I didn't want to be bothered. Spending most of my time in solitude meant nothing terrible could happen, and nobody could hurt me.

I spent my free time around campus sitting under various trees in the courtyard with my notebook and pen. There, I'd spill out my words, and the paper would love them. I had a guy come over and sit down next to me. "What ya writing?" The nerve. Who the heck is he, coming out of nowhere and being so damn nosy? He looked over and tried to take a peek at my notebook.

I held it against my chest. "I'm writing about stuff, and it's my stuff. I don't let anyone see my stuff."

The guy looked like a washed-up porn star from the '80s, complete with a thick, unruly mustache and feathered hair to match. "My name is Rich. Saw a pretty girl sitting by herself and couldn't let that happen."

"Yeah, hi. I'm Alex, and I'm not interested." Thank the good Lord he got up and walked away. My skin was crawling.

As it turns out, we had a class together the next semester. Oh, great. Of course, my brain went to the most illogical thought. Washed-up porn guy is a stalker. He's taking this class on purpose just to harass me. Yep, that must be it.

And Rich sat down right next to me, confirming my thoughts. "Hey! Remember me?"

I wished I hadn't. Oh well, he was in my class, but I could get over it. It was my first college writing class, and I was excited to start, Rich or no Rich.

He breezed into the room
an air of arrogance trailing behind.
Thick. Suffocating.

As I shared a snippet of my first piece of creativity, a certain someone took it to be about him, and his face turned sour. After class, he followed me out to my car, which I hadn't known until I went to put my key in my car door. Someone latched onto my right arm and spun me around.

"What the fuck, Rich? Let go of me."

"What was that shitty poem about?"

I was yelling louder now for him to let go of me. A guy a few cars down heard me scream and told Rich to get the hell away from me. Rich called me a crazy bitch and walked away. I withdrew from that writing class the next day and said fuck it to the writing stuff, because every time I shared, it just made people mad.

I sought out my savior right after dropping that writing class, so I could thank him. He told me to think nothing of it, that he would have done it for anyone, but to me, it was huge. Nobody ever came to my rescue before, even if my red flags were flying all over creation, not a single person, aside from Grandma, had ever swooped me up to protect me from anything. Immediately, I was attached.

My savior wasn't all that interesting. He had a crummy old Duster, wore beat-up Puma sneakers held together at the toes with a stretch of silver duct tape, looked like his mama dressed him, and had an ex he talked about ad nauseam. *Ex* is the word I honed in on. If he had an ex, it meant he was single. He wasn't my type, but he was single, and I was an equal opportunity kind of girl.

I came on strong like Rich the stalker, popping up all over campus for the next several days, pretending that I was just running into him. I wanted him to see me, to notice me, and to pay attention to me, and I wanted to make my presence known, be a force he couldn't possibly ignore. I played up my dress, hair, and make-up. One afternoon, I found him in the parking lot of the school, head under the hood of his smoking Duster, cursing at it to the moon and back.

It was my stunning opportunity to swoop in and save his day. "Hey! You need a ride?"

"Yeah, I guess that will be ok. I was going to call my mom, but she's at work, and I'd rather not bother her if I don't have to." Call his mom, how cute.

Two weeks later, I was pregnant. I'd like to say that we broke up two days after walking out of Planned Parenthood, but we would have been together first before we could have broken up. And if you're wondering what his name is, I've been trying to figure that one out for the last twenty-five years.

Twenty

MY STOMACH LEFT MY BODY THE FIRST TIME I SAW
those two blue lines creep across that test strip. I cried my eyes out
on the cold tile of the bathroom floor, and they weren't tears of joy
streaming down my face. I was eighteen years old, and I was terrified because I was knocked up by a guy who had no name, and I
knew I'd have to tell my parents just in case he bailed.

A flurry of bad ideas flooded my spinning head. From there, I
went into complete darkness. It was as if I was watching the entire
thing unfold from somewhere else, from some other vantage point,
from a body that was not my own. I shut down and disassociated.
My only defense was to detach, so I didn't have to feel the hurt, the
pain, the fear, or the anger that was boiling up inside me.

I had no idea that detaching had become instinct to me, a survival skill I had learned very early. It's relatively common in alcoholics to avoid anything painful, anything scary, anything that might
hurt. We withdraw, we block it out, we build walls so high nobody

can scale them, and then we hide behind them. We float in, out, and above our bodies. I had done this several times in my life up until this point, but this was the first time I was recognizing what I was doing. I knew I was in flight mode—running, shutting down, and paralyzed by fear.

I called Jennie. "What the fuck do you mean you're pregnant? Are you fucking stupid?"

I hung up. So much for Jennie. I never spoke to her again. I decided after that miserable phone call, I'd just tell my mother. I figured telling mom was far safer than telling my father. I couldn't tell him a damned thing without him blowing up on me. There in the kitchen, her back to me bent over a sink full of dishes, I went to her. She didn't even turn around, just kept on washing those stupid dishes. In a hushed voice, I heard her mumble, "You'll be the one to tell your father." Fuck.

I went to my father that night as he was sitting in bed watching *Wheel of Fortune*, sucking on a Marlboro Light. I had imagined the worst-case scenarios as I always had. He's going to throw me out. He'll never speak to me again. He'll hate me. He'll disown me. His reaction was far worse than that. I sat down on the edge of the bed and began to cry. Dad was staring at the TV, watching someone land on *bankrupt*.

My mother had told him already because before I could even speak, he did. He grabbed his pack of cigarettes, reaching for another, even though the one in the ashtray was still smoldering. "So, my daughter is a slut." He blew out a smoky plume that stung my eyes. I got off the bed, went into my bedroom, and closed the door. Dad's hurt came out as anger, and I deserved his reaction. I was the one who threw myself at this guy. I was the one who was so desperate for someone to love me that I took up with some guy I found to be the most uninteresting person I had ever met. I was the slut. I was the whore. I was what my father had said of me. I was that person. I was disgusting.

Later that night, when everyone was asleep, I took a knife from the kitchen drawer and carved up my arm. I needed release, and mutilating my body was the only way I thought I could escape. My mother took me to lunch the following day to discuss what I was planning on doing. I simply said it would all work out somehow.

I honestly hadn't given any thought to being a mother. I did have some fantasy in my head that my baby was a girl, and I'd do my best to provide her with what I didn't have. How foolish. I couldn't even pay for my clothing. I was eating my parents' food, using their water and electricity, and sleeping under their roof with absolutely no thoughts as to what my future would be.

"You will *not* have this baby," my mother said.

"That's ok. What's-his-name said he didn't want to be a dad." As it turned out, his ex wasn't an ex at all. He was still with her, and I was just a piece of ass on the side.

This time I opened my legs to a doctor who would remove the life that was inside of me. I wouldn't be a mother at lunchtime. Problem solved. I could forget and continue with my life as if this never happened. It was just a minor hiccup, a bump in the road, and everything would be ok if I just walked with my chin up and pretended everything was *hunky-dory*.

Twenty-One

I HAD SPENT THE NEXT SEVERAL WEEKS ALONE IN MY bedroom. I didn't want anyone to bother me, and nobody did. I wasn't eating. I wasn't talking. There was relatively no sign of me even living in that house at all. I felt like a ghost that nobody could see, floating around the four other lives in that house, and I liked it that way. The act of disappearing was my favorite.

When I did become visible, nobody asked me how I was. Nobody asked me how I was doing or how I felt. Everyone was going about their lives as if my abortion never happened. It was just a small smudge on the screen that could be easily wiped away with a quick dusting, leaving the picture flawless again. I was dumbfounded. I couldn't figure out why I was the only one devastated. How awful are these people? Can't they see my pain? Didn't anyone care about my suffering? If they did, they sure didn't show it. I decided I would move out. These people were fucked up.

I had no clue how I was going to execute my plan. I just wanted out, and that was good enough for me. I'd figure out the details along the way. My most brilliant idea was to meet a guy, make him fall in love with me, and get him to marry me somehow and then problem solved. Genius! I was now on a mission to get the hell out of my parents' house. Their era of ruling over me was going to come to an end, no matter what I had to do.

My thinking had gone off the rails at this point. When I was ready to go back to school, I didn't care what guy I found. I didn't care what he looked like, where he was from, or what his interests were. I didn't want to know families and didn't care what kind of car he drove, where he lived, or what color skin he had. If he was smart, that was a plus, but if he was stupid, I could overlook it. I didn't care if he was on drugs or infected with some sort of life-threatening disease. I wanted *out* and I didn't care who I'd have to latch onto to get me there.

On the first day of the fall semester, I sat in my Psychology 101 class and scanned the room for a victim. A good-looking guy with stunning green eyes and a faded Seminoles hat caught my eye, and he happened to catch mine staring right at him. Good enough. The next day I sat behind him, wondering how the hell I'd strike up a conversation with him. I honestly didn't know how to talk to anybody. I'll pass him a note, just like I did in high school. Let's see if that does the trick.

I think you're cute. What are you up to this weekend?

He turned around and smiled. "I think I'll go out with you."

Score! Well, I had to keep my options open, so I spread myself out everywhere in case this guy didn't pan out. I shopped for men at work, at the gas station, in the library, at the store. It didn't matter. Married men, older men, gay men I thought I could turn straight; nothing was off-limits. By twenty, I had figured out how to get men and very quickly. If one of them didn't work out, I had a long line of others just outside my door. I'd always have someone, of that I made sure. This girl was never going to be alone in the world. Flash a smile, lower my shirt, and I got ya.

I had Green Eyes, the night shift janitor at work, the married man, and a guy who was a girl, and I was dating them all. Of my prospects, Green Eyes was the most promising. I liked the janitor just fine because he left joints in my work locker. I wanted the married guy because there was no chance of him ever leaving his wife. And the guy who was a girl, well, there was no chance of another unwanted pregnancy, but I liked Green Eyes the best. He was in school, he had aspirations, his family had tons of money, and I just happened to be his very first girlfriend. The situation couldn't be more perfect. I could mold this guy into everything I wanted.

I had become a master of the art of subtle manipulation. I say *subtle* because if you're good at it, people will never know what you're doing, and you'll get your way every single time. Manipulation is nothing but disgusting, selfish behavior and not something I recommend, but it was the only way I could get what I wanted and needed so desperately.

I had no idea how to go about life otherwise. I didn't know how to tell anyone how I felt, why I felt it, what I needed, or why I needed it. I didn't know how to talk to people and when I did, I was continually questioning their motives, assessing their words, and finishing up conversations with conversations inside my head about how we'd never be friends because I was so closed off.

Feelings were things for soft people, and I was anything but soft. Words that people used to communicate feelings were utterly foreign to me unless they were spilling across the paper. Babies cry, losers complain, and only well-off people are happy. I honestly could not relate to anyone who cried, had little patience for people who moaned about their problems, and had absolutely no time for small talk. I did my best to copy people like an alien would copy a human to blend into society. It would be how I'd spend the next couple of decades—lying, cheating, and mastering manipulation to survive in a world that seemed foreign to me.

Twenty-Two

SWEET GREEN EYES. PERHAPS THE MOST SINCERE,
loving, generous person I had met up until that point in my life. He
loved me, and I knew it, but I walked all over him the entire four
years we were together like you'd walk on a carpet, only my shoes
were dirty, and his carpet was as white as snow.

Our relationship built itself upon a foundation of manipulation.
As the bricks that built the house of our young lives began to rise,
the mortar had noticeable cracks. Although cracks didn't matter because the walls stood fortified with what I was able to emulate by
watching other relationships around me. I was going to get this guy
to marry me. I'd make it so.

Green Eyes was quiet, shy, and loved to smoke weed, which was
perfectly fine with me since I was enjoying the occasional smoke,
or two, thanks to the night shift janitor. Still, I could swear Green
Eyes was addicted because as soon as he came down from his high,
he went right back up again, and it was constant. Our very first

phone conversation went a little bit like this: "So uh…do you smoke weed?"

"Sometimes."

"Ah, sweet! A cool chick." And thus began my love affair with drugs.

The only drugs off-limits to me, at the time I had decided, was meth, crack, and heroin. I had heard horrible, tragic things about them, and it scared the shit out of me. The gravity bong, though, I hit that something awful. I was smitten, and so was Green Eyes. Not only did I smoke weed, but I took hits like a grown-up. There I sat, day after day, in a dark and stuffy apartment going up just as soon as I came down. Green Eyes's friends were just as amazed by me as he was. "She's a keeper," one of them coughed.

I could not believe how much marijuana had become such an integral part of our lives. I am pretty sure I was high the entire four years of our relationship because everything we did surrounded it. We did absolutely nothing sober. We woke up and got high, at lunchtime we were high, and then a nap and high again. Dinner rolled around, and we were high, and on date nights we were exceptionally, almost nonfunctional high. My favorite part of being high was the feeling that I had finally fit in somewhere.

I was in the cool crowd for sure now. Everyone loved me. I kicked ass in video games, watched college football, and could keep up with their level of smoke. Some of my best memories of that relationship with Green Eyes was sitting around all day on Sunday, getting high, and playing *Super Puzzle Fighter II Turbo* on the Sony PlayStation. I was so good at that game that Green Eyes would invite everyone he knew to come over and try to beat me. To this day, I remain undefeated. What an accomplishment.

The higher I got, the better I became at everything I did. My writing was more creative, and any food I made could have come from any fine-dining establishment. I was funny, witty, and incredibly relaxed all the damned time. I enjoyed how drugs made me feel. Everything I did was always enhanced, and any anxiety or cares that I had just melted away. Every so often, a bad batch would come along, and things did melt away, faces especially. I had fallen in love with weed, and I think I had also fallen in love with Green Eyes.

I was the *cool chick* now, the one everyone wanted to be around. Green Eyes bragged about me to anyone who would listen. I overheard Green Eyes tell his brother that he had never wanted to get married, but maybe I was changing his mind. On the same beach where I had chosen to be homeless during that ill-fated prom weekend, Green Eyes proposed to me. I had done it. I'd gotten what I wanted, and I told everybody I knew that I was getting married. I was happy. Green Eyes was not. "Why are you telling everyone we're getting married? I'm not ready for the world to know about this." He stomped out his Marlboro Red. "You know I'm transferring schools this fall, and I honestly don't know where that will take us."

Shit. This fall was just a few short weeks away. Then what?

My wheels started to spin off course again. Green Eyes's leaving was personal; it had to be. I had made my mind up that he was changing colleges to get away from me. I told myself I had been too overbearing, too happy, too excited, and too *cool*, and now he was done. I had made it all about me instead of stopping even for one second to consider that a better school meant better opportunity for him.

I complained about it constantly. "But you're going to go away, and I'll be stuck here. You'll find someone else. I just know it." How pathetic I sounded. How insecure, selfish, and self-seeking. He relented and told me we'd be just fine. He'd only be two hours away, but in my mind, two hours away was as far as two planets away.

We managed a year while he was away, but I had become increasingly dependent, controlling, possessive, and jealous. I called him nonstop to check up on what he was doing. I knew he wanted me to back off and give him space, but I could never give it to him. I could only think of myself and how this separation was affecting me. The truth was I just didn't want Green Eyes to leave me. I applied to the same school and got accepted.

My expectations were not met. The day I moved into my dorm room, he dropped in to tell me we needed a break. My parents had tried to talk me out of following Green Eyes to this school, but I paid no attention. I wanted what I wanted. Now, I certainly could not pick up the phone crying, because I knew the only words I would hear out of my parents' mouths would be "I told you so."

I was sick to my stomach those first few weeks of school, feeling abandoned to navigate this new life where I didn't know a single person. I hated my roommate, I had noisy neighbors that partied all night, and Green Eyes wasn't returning any of my calls. I was alone, and that was terrifying. There was no choice but to get involved, or I knew how things would end. I'd spend my days in bed feeling sorry for myself, or I'd leave that school and go home.

I set out to make friends and found a coed honors fraternity. I had a 3.5 GPA, so why not rush? I needed a place to belong, assimilate, and find my place, and maybe this would be it. When I received my letters, I soon found that this organization was different from the rest of the Greek groups on campus. One thing remained the same: the mixers where a few sororities and fraternities got together to *mix*. Just because we were nerds didn't mean we weren't invited to go get our red Solo cups and drink with the rest of them. These parties were massive alcohol-induced hookup parties. Landing guys there would be easy since everyone was there looking for the same thing: sex.

Put me in a room full of testosterone and booze and I'd light myself on fire for attention. Alcohol in my body would have me planning who I'd take back to my dorm in a matter of an hour, or less. Green Eyes wanted me to find a life of my own, and that's what I had set out to do. Fuck you, buddy. I bet plenty of guys would love a shot at me. On the inside resided hurt, anger, and loneliness. I just didn't care anymore, and alcohol, I had learned, made me care even less. The more I drank, the less I'd feel, and it eventually made me not care at all.

What a fantastic tool alcohol was. It was solving all of my problems. I was quickly making friends now because alcohol made me feel more relaxed and social. I'd get the guys I wanted because they saw how fun and carefree I was. It was like moths to a flame. Alcohol meant an instant good time, but there was still the issue of learning how to drink. The only way I knew was to drink until I either got sick or passed out, and that was a problem.

There had to be some sort of skill to learn to avoid that. My parents, as much as they drank, rarely got sick. When my dad drank too much, he got belligerent. When Mom drank too much, she just went up to bed. What was my limit? When did I have to stop? It

took a few parties and a handful of one-night stands to get it all figured out. Three drinks were my limit. Any more than that, and I'd
be flat on my back or peeing behind a building somewhere and not
remembering how I got home.

Twenty-Three

I HAD FINALLY ARRIVED AT THE PLACE I WANTED TO be. I had fun friends, more guys than I could have ever imagined, an organization that I loved belonging to, and best of all I was out from underneath my parents' reign. I had grown up. I was free.

As soon as Green Eyes caught wind of my new life, he wanted to try again. I dropped everything and ran back. After all, he was my meal ticket to stability after college. Sure, I was living the good life now, but I did have to start thinking about my future because college was soon coming to an end. I still had no idea what I wanted to do with my life, aside from land a husband. Nobody had much faith in my abilities while I was growing up, so I figured my safest bet was to *marry rich*, as my dad had suggested. I hitched my rope around Green Eyes' star once again.

I had decided to tie my rope rather loosely this time or risk losing Green Eyes again. I knew for sure that I had to keep faking this new form of myself that I had adopted to make him happy. If

I could solidly convince Green Eyes that I had everything figured out, he'd keep me around. I wouldn't be as needy this time; I'd be less attached and act like I wouldn't care if he was around or not. I'd do whatever I thought was necessary to keep him around this time. I was desperate for someone to love me.

I was the new, improved fiancé. I rarely called him, gave him his space, and let the chips fall where they may. When he asked me if I wanted to go out somewhere, I'd make up an elaborate story about how I already had these fantastic plans with my friends. Green Eyes was going to live with my terms of agreement now. I'd see you when I wanted to.

Little did he know, I rarely had plans at all. I had dropped everything for him. My friends all took a back seat, I stopped going to my organization's weekly meetings, and I left the party scene. I had no plans. He was my plan, but I couldn't let him know that. It was just another game I had decided I would play in an endless effort to have love and attention. My goal was to get him to miss having me around. I wanted him to be jealous. It was a ridiculous plan, but it was working.

We went back home together to visit our families one weekend, and while we were there, he decided that he needed me to be around more. Ah, perfect! But for some reason, I wouldn't have it. After I had him in my net, I realized that I didn't want him. I couldn't understand. I had worked so hard, manipulated the crap out of him, then decided I wasn't interested. I got up to the goal line and froze when it was time to make the touchdown. I wanted to go back to my partying lifestyle. It was fun. I didn't want to settle down; maybe I just wanted to see if I could get there if I wanted.

We went back to school, and I continued to do my own thing, but my partying increased tenfold. My train was leaving the rails, and I could see it but didn't care. I continued to meet random guys in a drunken haze, hooking up with them for a night and pretending the next day when I saw them on campus that I had no idea who they were. The truth was sometimes I didn't. The last thing I remembered sometimes was sitting on a barstool, doing shots, and coming to the next day, not remembering who I was with, how I got back to my room, or what had happened in between the bar and waking up without my clothes.

I was ashamed, but I would just drink to forget about how bad I felt on the inside. Sometimes I'd sit in my room alone and wonder where a life of drinking, drugging, and sleeping around with strangers was going to lead. I imagined a life of prostitution or being a drunk in a gutter, chugging down her breakfast from a brown paper bag. All the roads I was on now were going nowhere. I saw my brother's life falling apart, and now mine was too. But I also knew that I was too smart to ever be that drunk in the gutter.

Then, I saw those two blue lines creep across another test strip. This time I had no idea who the father was. It probably happened during one of my blackouts, for all I knew. I referred to the list I had kept of the guys I had remembered sleeping with. I thought, is this fucking normal to keep a list like this? Probably not, but it was handy. I figured if I had wound up murdered, at least there'd be a list of suspects.

I was royally fucked this time. How could I have been so reckless? My roommate felt so sad for me on so many levels. She was watching me fall further and further into a hole, and there was nothing she, or anyone, could do but watch me tumble face-first into mess after mess.

"You know, it's one thing to fuck around with your own life, but now you're fucking around with other people's lives. The worst part is that you don't even care. What kind of person are you?" she asked.

I hated people who told me the truth.

After a couple of weeks of sleuthing, I had finally figured out who it was. It was the guy from my Wednesday night rhetoric class. We went over to the bar on our fifteen-minute break from our three-hour class to do shots, and we never went back. I woke up the next morning not remembering a damned thing. A girl from my hall had stopped me to ask if I was seeing someone new because she had seen me bringing a guy back to my room one night a couple of weeks ago.

"Nah, I'm not seeing him." Bingo. I had my answer.

I was going to tell Green Eyes it was his baby when I knew damned well it wasn't. I hadn't slept with him in weeks, but it was my best option. The two of us were so blasted; I doubted the guy from my class remembered our night together either.

Green Eyes had graduation in a matter of weeks, and I knew that what I was about to do was the most horrible thing, but I had no choice. He took me to dinner one night, and I laid it on him over our cheeseburgers. "I'm pregnant."

His face went white. He grabbed a hold of my hand and told me not to worry. We'd figure it out. When we worked up the nerve to tell his parents (not mine) that we were expecting, his mom was thrilled. "Oh my God! That's wonderful." Sigh. I began to cry, and she held me in her arms. Again, these were not tears of happiness. This woman had no idea this was not her grandchild.

The guilt I felt was unbearable. I was the most disgusting, lowest human being on the face of the earth. What had I done? Now Green Eyes and his parents both had been deceived. Green Eyes's mom continued. "What do your parents think about this?" she asked, her tender voice cracking.

"Well, I haven't told them yet." I knew how they'd react and what they'd say. When I got back to my dorm that Sunday night, I called home.

Thank God it was my mother who answered and not my father. My voice began to shake, and tears began to well up in the corners of my eyes. I sighed into the phone. "Hi, Mom."

She didn't say hello back. "Oh, let me guess. You're pregnant again." The tone she took made it seem like I was getting knocked up every month. Although I should have expected it, her response was so matter-of-fact, so cold, so hurtful. She continued. "We're not telling your father this time. Get rid of it." And she hung up the phone.

Another brilliant idea drummed up in my mind: I'll keep this baby to spite her. But damn, the gig would be up when the baby arrived eight months later, half-white and half–African American. No, Mom was right. I had to get rid of *it*. Ultimately, I convinced Green Eyes that we couldn't have this baby, not now. He had an entire life ahead of him with a promising career lined up, and I didn't want to burden him with having to take care of a baby. Ultimately, he agreed, and I made an appointment.

As we arrived at the appointment, a group of angry pro-life protestors yelled at us from the car all the way to the front door. Green Eyes got the worst of it. "What kind of father are you to kill your child? You're a murderer!" My guilt deepened. He shouldn't be the target. The entire scene was of my doing. I was the reason he was here. I was the problem. "Murderers! Murderers! You're going to hell." Well, now that I was a target, too, I felt much better.

After the procedure, both of us walked back to our car in tears. Green Eyes was crying over the loss of his baby, and I was a sobbing mess for being the lying, cheating, child-killing murderer that I was. God, if He were there, would never forgive me for this, and I would never, ever forgive myself. I was truly horrible, the lowest of the low. I hated everything that I had become. When he dropped me back off at my dorm, I laid down on my bed and stayed there for three days.

The phone rang. It was my mother. No how are you, or how are you feeling, just one question. "Did you do as I said?"

"Yeah, Mom, I did." I hung up the phone and laid back down on the bed. I wanted to die. I didn't know what else to do anymore. Was this what life was? An endless string of pain and punishment? My cramps were unbearable, I was bleeding fiercely, and I had a headache from crying for three days straight. Fuck this. I grabbed the bottle of Motrin that was sitting on my desk and swallowed the entire bottle with a half a bottle of vodka. I'm out.

I woke up in a hospital with a tube down my throat and the blackened contents of my stomach pumping out into a bag. I was pissed that I couldn't even kill myself right. I tried ripping the tube out of my throat and wound up sedated. The next time I woke up, I was upstairs in the mental ward. I had been committed.

I'd like to say I was a resident there for a while because I knew I belonged there, but I was only on a seventy-two-hour hold. My mom drove six hours up to the hospital to bring me back home with her. It was the last place I wanted to be, but what the hell choice did I have any more? I tried to off myself. I was batshit crazy.

I sat alone in the common room in a corner chair while I waited for my mother. I convinced myself that I wasn't nearly as bad as the people who were there with me in the looney bin. There was an older man in too long of a white robe and white plastic slippers pacing back and forth across the room, having a conversation with someone I couldn't see. There was a girl around my age with bandages wrapped around both of her wrists, mumbling softly to herself as she stared into a TV that wasn't on. And there was a middle-aged woman sitting on the floor, rocking a baby doll. These people are fucking crazy. I gave zero thought to being right there along with them, just as insane as the day is long. Mom finally got there just as I was about to take my *supervised* shower. Oh, thank God.

When I got back to my parents' house, my brother was sitting in the kitchen, sucking on a cigarette. "I heard you tried to off yourself. It looks like you failed." Ah, yes, I was home. I spent the next three months cemented to the living room couch. The psychiatrist at the hospital had put me on such a cocktail of drugs that it rendered me useless. I couldn't even manage to go upstairs to my bed. So I laid there, a complete zombie, dead to the world and unfeeling, eating, watching TV, and sleeping.

I remember Green Eyes calling to check up on me, and I couldn't bring myself to talk to him. I was still being eaten alive on the inside by my guilt; that was the one thing I could feel. Eventually, he stopped calling, and good old Green Eyes slowly became an ugly stain on the slate of who I was. I felt somewhat relieved that Green Eyes was behind me, but letting go of this part of my life was going to be riddled with claw marks. I had to force myself to close the book on him, move on, and never look back.

Twenty-Four

MY PARENTS EVENTUALLY GOT TIRED OF LOOKING AT me anchored to their couch and told me to get off my ass and do something with my life. I gathered up my pieces and set out to find myself once again. My brother had told me about this new thing called AOL and that I could use it to talk to and meet new people, and that's exactly what I needed to make my brand new start.

I needed people. I needed new people. All of the ones I had known erased themselves from my memory. My college friends now knew that I had had a stint in a mental hospital, so I didn't bother reaching out to any of them. I was a certified head case. I figured I'd take my brother's advice. Besides, if I could find friends online, that meant no more awkward starter conversations. I could have a drink, or two, before reaching out, so I could have the courage to say hello.

Of course, what I wanted was a guy. I had screwed up every relationship I had up until this point, and since my parents had moved a few states away, at twenty-three, I could create an entirely new life with no questions asked. I was starting to see my life as a series of chapters out of a horror story. I flipped the page to a blank one and began to write again.

There I was, stuck in my parents' house again, the last place I wanted to be. So I hopped online and started to scour the internet in search of a completely different life. Dad walked by. "Hey, while you're sitting there, why don't you look for a job too."

I ignored him and went about creating the best online dating profile that I could. Two hours later, "You've got mail." My inbox was full. I sat there with a glass of chardonnay and sorted through my prospects. I narrowed it down to ten.

My parents were shocked about how quickly I was moving around again. Why shouldn't I be? I had quit taking my medication a week ago. I was tired of dragging myself around like there was a hundred-pound weight chained around my ankles and my head feeling like it was stuck inside of an empty fishbowl.

I was parading men in and out of my parents' house like there was a revolving door out front. I had so many men lined up for myself that I had to lighten my load a bunch. Crooked teeth? Next. You live in your mom's basement, and you're thirty-five? Next. Fuck! You don't drink? *Next!* Eventually, I had it narrowed down to five, and I was having the time of my life with them all.

There was the wealthy divorcé *GQ* model, the NCIS dude who looked a heck of a lot like Ray Liotta, Mr. Drinky who was six foot five and a prominent attorney in the city, Tiny Shoes, and a cute blond Navy guy who had graduated high school the same year I did. I had also gotten myself a part-time job at the mall to appease my father and get him off my back. Unfortunately for him, I had decided not to go back to school.

GQ was devastatingly gorgeous. He always looked like he had just stepped off the cover of a magazine. He was always tan, his teeth were piano key–white, and he never had a single hair out of place on his pretty little head. He bragged about all of his modeling jobs, and although I never did see an actual magazine spread, he had giant blown-up framed photos of himself plastered all over his house. Even in his bathroom there was a sixteen-by-twenty painted portrait of him sitting in a little white sailboat out in the middle of a body of water somewhere, dressed in a white polo shirt, dark blue Dockers, and white and blue boat shoes. In his left hand was an oar. The other hand held a martini glass with two olives on a toothpick. Next to him on the seat of the boat was a bottle of gin. His overly white teeth flashed a sly smile.

GQ had specific rules for dating that I never quite figured out, aside from the feeling that he was most likely married, and I was a side chick. We could only see each other on Tuesday and Thursday nights after 6:00 p.m., never on the weekends, and there was no staying overnight at his house. I was never to call him, and he would call me. Fair enough. You are probably far past Mr. Wrong, but you're pretty, so I'll keep you until I get bored.

NCIS dude annoyed the living shit out of me. He tried too hard, had Fatboy Slim repeatedly playing on full blast in his red Geo Metro, and lived in a tiny studio apartment that had a couch, a bed, and a table. On the table sat piles and piles of manila folders stuffed to burst with papers and photos. I looked at NCIS dude as he was sitting on the couch, dancing to some imaginary song in his head. I thought, damn, this one is going to be one hell of a project. It meant I could help him make improvements. But was it going to be worth the amount of time I would have to give? The only thing the guy had going for him was his stable career with the Navy Criminal Investigation Service, and he seemed to love it. "Man, there is nothing quite like catching bad guys in our military, let me tell you." And he would sit there telling me story after story, which I'm reasonably sure he wasn't supposed to be doing half the time. I'll call him when I'm bored.

Mr. Drinky, the lawyer, was another breed entirely. I had never seen anyone drink so much in one sitting and still be functional. What a marvel. I wish I could do that. Oh, and he was handsome. He wasn't *pretty handsome* like GQ but manly looking handsome. He towered above my tiny five-foot-four, 110-pound frame. His shadow would blot out the sun when he stood next to me. He owned his own home on the beach, drove a beautifully restored first-year Firebird, and had been married before, but that was no matter; I didn't want to marry a drunk. Besides, when he introduced me to his friends, he introduced me as his "next future ex-wife."

Aside from the facts, there's not much more to say about him. Neither of us was attached to the other and perfectly ok with the arrangement just to have sex occasionally. I could live with that. After about a month of it, I put Mr. Drinky and all his barfly friends back up on the shelf with the rest of the shot glasses. The sex wasn't even good; I was surprised I never fell asleep during it.

Tiny Shoes had nothing *tiny* about him. He was six foot six and roughly 380 pounds. He earned his name because of the mysterious five pairs of size-five Asian house slippers that were lined up just on the inside of his front door. Maybe he ran a massage parlor. He was a drug dealer and didn't even try to hide it. People were always coming and going and only staying long enough to watch the scale and hand over wads of cash. A quick internet search of the guy immediately brought up a mugshot. Yep, he had a felony drug charge that landed him in prison for a bit. Well, I won't be taking this one home to Mom and Dad, but at least I know where I could get drugs if I wanted them.

I made a near-fatal error one night, hanging out with him at his house. "Hey, I got some extra shrooms here for us. Are ya interested?" he asked.

"Let me think a bit. The last time I went on a trip, I wound up standing in a closed-door, dark bathroom for two hours waving a glow stick in the mirror, sat staring at a black light poster of Jimi Hendrix on the wall for the next couple of hours, and then I lost a chunk of about eighteen hours that I've been unable to recover. Sure, let's do it," I said.

"Awesome. I got some leftover pizza in the refrigerator. We can throw the mushrooms on top because I know they can be a little harsh, especially if you don't like mushrooms."

We should have stayed home, but I wanted to see the movie *Titanic*. Big mistake. I was doing all right until Rose's face kept coming apart in molecules and going back together again. When the boat started taking on water after it hit that iceberg, I got seasick. I climbed over the mountain that was Tiny Shoes and ran for a black-and-white-checkered bathroom. Fuck. This once tastefully decorated bathroom was now covered in a giant puddle of cheese and mushroom bits.

I didn't even tell Tiny Shoes I was leaving. Like the biggest dummy in the world, I got in my car and drove through what I truly believed was a video game but what was just the I-64 tunnel. It's a miracle I didn't die that night. I got to my bed and slept for twenty-two hours. I didn't think it was a good idea to see Tiny Shoes or his massage parlor anymore. Lastly, was tall, blond, good-looking Navy guy who was starkly different from the other cast of characters. Even though I could see through the bullshit of his AOL ad, I found him intriguing. My AOL ad was bullshit too. I hadn't liked the New York Giants or the New York Knicks since I was ten years old, but I was intriguing also, in my unique way. The most significant difference between him and the others was that I wanted to learn about him.

PART II

Twenty-Five

SUMMER, 2019

I'M SITTING IN MY FRONT PORCH HAMMOCK, DRINKING my morning cup of liquid energy, and watching Navy repair another busted sprinkler head that had turned into Old Faithful. Our kids are older now, and our daughter is about to leave for college. We'll still have the boys here, but I know the house will be a lot less vibrant without her.

It feels like only a minute or two have gone by since we brought these four kids into this world—not two decades. Navy and I were so young, so full of hope, and looked forward brightly upon dedicating a significant portion of our lives to raising them to be good humans.

The four of them may argue incessantly over who has to do the dishes, who let the dogs out last, and who mowed over the last cushion from my backyard patio set, leaving the stuffing for our golden retriever who made the yard look like a giant teddy bear exploded. Still, they are the loves of my lifetime. They came from God and belong to God, and I'm the one God chose to raise them.

Two years ago, Navy and I were on the brink of divorce, and then again one year ago, we were on the verge of divorce. I'm not sure if we have brought it back yet from the brink, because things are still not as good as they could be. I had done what many people would consider definite *deal breakers*. I had never been the greatest wife, but in the last few years, I had been a downright terrible one.

Twenty-Six

SUMMER, 1999

WE WERE TALKING ON THE PHONE FOR HOURS AT A time. Given my track record of finding the very worst men possible, I approached Navy just a little bit differently than the rest by spending a reasonable amount of time getting to know him before jumping into the sack with him.

I was playing cute with this guy, allowing him to discover and learn about me by asking questions. Typically, I threw myself at anything that was breathing, so maybe doing the opposite of everything I had done in the past would work better for me. That plan lasted about three days because by then the phone calls were enough, and we agreed to meet.

Navy peered over the top of his *Maxim* magazine as he sat waiting for me on a bench just outside the store in the mall where I was working. All the girls I was working with were curious about the cute blond guy who kept looking at me. "I've never seen a picture of him, but I think that's my date."

Two aisles down, one of my coworkers yelled, "Hey, if it doesn't work out, would you give me his number?"

My eyes narrowed. I yelled back, "I saw him first." It was like I was back in middle school. But who knew? Maybe this is *the one*. Lord knows I had kissed my share of frogs.

I was crazy. I *knew* I was crazy. I had plenty of doctors who told me I was, but for me to think that Navy could be *the one* was a whole different level of crazy. Calm the fuck down and just enjoy yourself. Navy would see just how cute I was in person. I was a tiny little blond thing with a sweet little job and a little beater of a car I called Green Bean, and I still slept in my cute little yellow bedroom with the blue trim. How could he resist all of that cuteness?

He had no idea that I had been a suicidal mental patient just months before with a drug and alcohol problem, or that I had been looking for someone to save me but had an awful, sick, and disturbing way with men who I typically just viewed as conquests. He didn't know anything about my homelife, that I had dropped out of school not once, not twice, but three times, and that I had no intention of ever going back. I was living my *new* life now. The other two I had tried on didn't fit. Navy, you're up at bat. He had no clue how many foul balls he'd have to field along the way.

Twenty-Seven

SUMMER, 2019

"MOM, CAN YOU TAKE MY FRIENDS AND ME DOWN TO the pool?" my oldest son asked, as he stood there in the kitchen wearing his swimsuit, a towel draped around his neck and goggles on top of his head. He knew I'd say yes. How could I refuse when he was standing there ready to go, the stinker. Besides, I was one of those *cool* moms that every kid wants.

Don't get me wrong. I'm not that kind of mom. I do have rules for my teens, although they are loose. School is your job, curfew is at 10:00 p.m., go to bed at a decent hour, and love one another. They weren't born with a set of directions, so I've tried my best to raise them into human beings that are good in this world. The world needs a heck of a lot more humans that are compassionate and have good hearts, self-confidence, and a strong sense of what is right and wrong. All of those things seem pretty easy to teach our tiny ones, but it takes a lot of work being strong when they can't be and leading by living the example in our own lives.

Navy and I had our first child when we were just twenty-five. Immediately, I thought her prematurity was God's punishment on me for being a murderer of the unborn. I didn't see her birth as a gift. It was payback, something I deserved. Navy and I were both shocked and terrified by her early entrance. All the doctors could ever tell us was "She's doing as we expect." This is my fault. This is all my fault. All I was able to focus on in those NICU days wasn't the beauty of my daughter, my precious gift from the Lord, but the *thwack-hiss* sound of the ventilator keeping her alive.

Now, I'm watching from my front porch as the minivan pulls away from the curb. My preemie is leaving for college in the fall, and I have no idea how it happened or how I'm going to live without her here. I raised her to be strong, independent, significant, selfless, and proud of herself. She is all of those things and a shining example of what it means to persevere. I'm proud of what God did with her, and although I'm sad she's leaving, I'm excited to see what His plans are. Our three boys will soon follow, and although it's a hard pill to swallow, the answer to remaining happy and grounded through it all is acceptance.

As I sit and reflect upon the blossoming lives God has entrusted me with, I see only hope because I know they are in His care, and the plan for them is His and not my own. That said, I didn't always see it through this lens. Having four kids, ages five and under, was no easy deal. I was nowhere near prepared for the amount of work that went into having four little humans. I merely thought that having such a big family would be so much fun.

Harder still was the fact that Navy and I lived in one of the most rural towns you can ever imagine near the northwest corner of Pennsylvania. The closest airport was two hours to our north, our church had fifteen active members, and the nearest Big Mac was a forty-minute drive.

It was me and the four littles while Navy busted his ass to support us. The amount of stress that brought upon me was crushing. It was our choice that I stay at home, but I had no idea that it would be something to which I'd sacrifice my entire life.

The only way to escape was in my bedroom with a glass of wine.

Twenty-Eight

SUMMER, 1999

DATING NAVY WAS A COMPLETE WHIRLWIND. IT WAS June of 1999 when we first locked eyes, locked lips, and sealed the deal that we were a couple. There was something about him that I couldn't quite put my finger on. He was hard to explain. I knew I wasn't getting the real guy. He was covering up the person he indeed was underneath with his air of arrogance, inflated sense of self-importance, and devastatingly good looks (not that I wasn't doing the same).

It was a case of both of us trying to fit a mold, the mold that we thought the other wanted, instead of just being ourselves, as if being ourselves was dangerous. We both wanted to be liked by the other. We wanted people to like us and fall in love with an idea, not a person. The real person inside remained buried deep within, wondering when and if it will be safe to come out.

My parents warned me about dating him. He was in the Navy, and from what I heard, it's common knowledge that Navy men are not men with which you want to settle down. My parents were convinced that he was no good and probably up to no good. He was a cheat and a liar and would just leave me brokenhearted. No, this guy wasn't to be trusted. What the hell did they know? My parents had zero experience and believed what they heard through TV or gossip. Of course, my parents' comments meant that I'd go after this guy harder than the others because I had taken up a cause. I had been trying to prove them wrong for years, convinced myself they didn't want to see me happy.

Throughout June, July, and August, we were inseparable. Whenever I felt like Navy was trying to create some distance, I tried even harder. I was after him, I wanted him, and I would make damned sure he wouldn't forget. It was borderline stalker behavior, and I had given him plenty of reason to run the hell the other way several times, but he didn't. For whatever reason, he was attracted to me too—just as smitten, just as intrigued as I was. Maybe he was also looking for *the one* and chose to ignore the red flags waving in the warm, humid southeastern Virginia winds.

After a few weeks of dating, I had worked up the nerve to bring him home, knowing well that this could be the end of us. Once he meets my family, he will run. Ain't no way he'll want to be a part of this. My brother was sitting there on my infirmary bed (also known as the living room couch), watching *Jerry Springer* and throwing back bottles of Budweiser at two in the afternoon. He flicked the long head of a cigarette into an overflowing ashtray on the coffee table and looked Navy up and down. "Hey, buddy. Want a beer?" my brother sloshed, as he lit up another Newport Light.

Navy's eyes narrowed, and his face twisted. "Nah, man. I'm good."

Great, just great. My family is no white-picket-fence kind of family. I went upstairs to change for our date, and my head immediately began to spin. What the hell is he thinking? What kind of reflection would he be on me? He was always trying to ruin shit for me. Things go great then he throws a banana peel out for me, watches me slip on it, and laughs. Oh no, he is *not* going to fuck things up for me this time.

It was yet another instance of my brain going from zero to a hundred in less than sixty seconds. From my brother asking my date if he wanted a beer, right to thinking that he was intentionally trying to ruin my life. Something as simple as "Want a beer?" spun me out and pissed me off. I thought for a hot minute that the doctor at the looney bin was right; I needed that drug cocktail. Then I came to my conclusion on the matter. I don't need any fucking crazy pills. Case closed.

Then Navy met my parents. Strike two! My parents had been hanging out at their favorite watering hole, watching baseball. I had come to learn, in the few short months I had been living back at home, that if they weren't at the house, I could find them at Toadies. Now why the hell I brought Navy over to Toadies, I had no idea. I guess I figured that both parents would be more relaxed and, therefore, more open to my new guy.

Navy and I walked hand in hand into the dank and dark strip mall bar to find my mom and dad, butts cemented to their stools, chatting mindlessly with someone named Donkey. My gut instinct was to turn around and hightail it out of there before I was spotted, but it was too late. I knew the look, sound, and smell of inebriation, and it hung in the air like a funnel cloud.

"Hey, muffin."

Sigh. "Hi, Dad," I croaked.

I sat down on the empty stool next to my mom. Navy stood behind me with his hand resting on my shoulder. Go. Go! Run. Leave. Never look back. Before I could even say a word about who was with me, I was interrupted.

"Oh, another one? That was quick." Ah, wonderful. Thanks, Mom. I knew alcohol made her loose, but seriously now. I ordered a glass of wine, then another. Something had to help me through this nonsense.

I took out my compact mirror and refreshed my make-up. My dad grabbed my purse and started shuffling through it, looking for what? No idea. He tossed it at me from across the bar, and it landed on the floor near Navy's feet. He picked up my purse and all of its spilled contents and sat them on top of the bar. All of my make-up was broken. I chugged the last of my drink and left, Navy following behind my flames of anger.

"Sorry about that. My parents aren't themselves when they drink. It's like a case of Jekyll and Hyde." I continued as Navy looked blankly toward his car. "They aren't usually like that," I lied. We climbed into Navy's electric-blue '92 Camaro and drove off to the beach half-drunk.

Twenty-Nine

SUMMER, 1999

NEAR THE END OF OUR WHIRLWIND SUMMER, NAVY and I started staying in instead of going out every night. He had run out of money, blowing it all on me. It didn't matter much. I enjoyed spending time with him no matter what we were doing. I was just as happy sitting in his apartment playing *Jeopardy* on the PlayStation as I was dancing at Bar Norfolk.

My head started to lie to me again. It was making up bullshit just as it always had. This time it was telling me Navy was too good to be true. There *had* to be something wrong with him. If he only knew who I was. If he knew the truth about me, if he knew my past, he'd hate me. There might not be anything wrong with him, but I knew for damned sure there was a laundry list of things wrong with me.

If, if, if. I had to tighten my grip before Navy found out about me. I didn't want him to leave. I had decided to keep my secrets just a little bit longer, and so I buried them even deeper in my body where no light could touch. My darkest, most shameful pieces would never see daylight. Everything would be *hunky-dory*, and then summer ended, and so did Navy's time in the service.

He was leaving all right; he secured a job six hundred miles away. I was just a casualty. I did somehow manage to make his leaving all about me, just as I always had. Sure, he said he was leaving for a job, but I couldn't help but think that I had been too much, too serious, too needy, too smothering, too everything. At the same time, I had also convinced myself that I wasn't enough to make him want to stay. I was too much and not enough. Navy was moving on toward his future, and I was still stuck here as a living piece of furniture in my parents' home.

I could not let go. Navy was my hope. He was the one who I had begun to love. He was my escape from everything awful, hateful, and shameful. With him, all transgressions would fade into oblivion. With him, I felt safe. Navy was my new life, but now he was leaving, too, just as everyone else had. I could not and would not let him go.

The less we talked, the more I tried to insert myself and find a way to make myself a permanent fixture in his life. He was a good ten hours away by car, and even at the age of twenty-three, I was still at home and headed in no direction. The pause button on my life was stuck. I sat on my parents' back deck, crying into my hands about what a pathetic, worthless, waste of oxygen I was. Then I called myself an asshole, walked up to my bedroom, packed a bag, got in my car, and drove up to Pennsylvania. On the kitchen counter, I left a note: Went to visit Navy for the weekend; I'll be back Monday.

It took fifteen hours to get there, with every road closed due to flooding from Hurricane Floyd. All I could think about was getting to Navy, and all of the washed-out roads in the world weren't going to stop me.

After an incredible weekend, in which Navy and I rarely left the hotel, I decided I would not be going home. I pitched the idea to Navy of my staying there with him full-time, and after admitting to me that the gene pool in northwestern Pennsylvania wasn't very promising, he agreed. I would be staying. Navy and I would be together and creating a life of our very own.

That Sunday, I called home. "Mom, I'm not coming back tomorrow."

"Uh, so when will you be back then?" she asked nervously.

"I'm not coming back, Mom." I hung up the phone.

The following weekend, Navy and I rented a U-Haul and drove back down to Virginia. My parents had packed up three sizeable black garbage bags and left them in the dining room. Mom was there to see me off, but Dad didn't want to see me or talk to me. "Your dad didn't want to be here," Mom chided.

"Yeah, well, I'm not surprised. He doesn't know how to act when things around him don't go his way." I acted like it was no skin off my nose, but inside I was hurt. What kind of dad does this? Couldn't he accept that I was an adult now? I wasn't his little girl in pigtails anymore, but sometimes I still needed to be.

Navy and I threw my bags of belongings into the truck and made a stop at the Salvation Army just outside of town. We knew we didn't have a pot to piss in and that we wouldn't be able to survive on God's good grace. The only place where we could afford anything was at a thrift store, which I felt was somehow below me. But what choice did we have? We bought a three-dollar broken green-floral upholstered rocker chair, ripped a *paid* sticker off a lamp, stuck it to a queen-size mattress, and walked out. Navy and I were on our way.

I had a little bit of apprehension about this big step in my life. It wasn't like me just to drop everything and run. But more than that, I was excited and hopeful for the future, even though it was terrifying to walk into the unknown with absolutely no life skills whatsoever. I was free of my father, and that was enough.

Ten hours later, Navy and I arrived back to our tiny hotel room in our little rural town that time forgot, and I began unpacking my three big black garbage bags. Clothing, some photos of my fake friends from my artificial life, and a thick stack of poetry. My writing! Mom must have done some deep digging in my bedroom to have found these. I suppose if she could sniff out my brother's hidden liquor bottles in the tank of the toilet, she could find my writing.

I went into a panic. The poems were all out of order. Mom sure had a lot of nerve shuffling through my secrets like this. I wasn't ready for anyone to read these. My writing was mine. These were *my* feelings, and nobody has a right to *my* feelings. The pain is mine. Hate swelled from somewhere deep inside. I had been severely violated.

I took my stack of writings and hid them again. God forbid Navy gets ahold of them. What would he think if he read them? Navy would then see just how broken a person I was. He'd see damaged goods. Who would want a life with damaged goods? Navy didn't deserve the person who I had been hiding. She had done tragic things, suffered, and didn't deserve someone so beautiful. He was too good for me, and I would spend half my life believing and living that lie.

Thirty

SUMMER, 2019

I HADN'T HEARD BACK FROM THE RESPONDING OFFI-cer on the vandalism report I had filed. I had his card and case number up on the refrigerator, even though I had absolutely no intention to call the officer back and follow up with him. Instead, the card just sat there under the Cancun, Mexico, magnet hanging out among various pictures of family, friends, and household bills coming due. Every time I opened the refrigerator door, I prayed over that card. "God, place your loving arms around this officer, my offender, and those suffering, that they may know you and accept your grace. Amen."

"I don't understand. Why aren't you doing more? How come you haven't followed up?" asked a friend of mine, irritated with my inaction on the matter, as I was pouring myself a cup of dried-up river-bottom coffee. Jeez, who made this shit today? I can stand my spoon upright in it.

"Well, I prayed on it every day for a week, and so far the only answer that came was that I should leave it alone. God will take care of it." I grabbed my Long John doughnut, found my seat, and silenced my phone.

Thirty-One

FALL, 1999

I FOUND US OUR VERY FIRST APARTMENT JUST DAYS before our time at the rinky-dink hotel in town was going to run out. It was an uninspiring two-story old mill worker's home near Hamlin Lake that was now two separate apartment units. We had the upstairs flat at $250 a month. It was a steal, but Navy and I still had trouble figuring out how we would pay the rent and eat at the same time.

I was still living on my parents' dime somewhat. When I took off for greener pastures, they hadn't completely cut me off. I still had my bipolar medications provided for because my parents were well aware of what would happen if I didn't have them. Even if my parents and I weren't on speaking terms, they made sure I had continued access to those. If not for *my* benefit but for the poor, un-suspecting soul that took up with me, I needed those medications.

Having dropped out of college due to my *medical emergency*, coupled with the fact that Navy and I lived in the middle of nowhere, job prospects were slim. There were jobs to be had. I could have worked a job at the bakery at 3:00 a.m., the local grocery store was hiring baggers, and the diner down the street was looking for help, but there was nothing there that made me stand up and declare to the world that I had found my calling. Navy had even gone as far as setting me up with a job at his company. Luckily, they didn't hold it against him when I decided that the job wasn't for me. Instead, I chose the avenue of full-time stay-at-home mom, and we went about making that happen.

It was a giant slap across the face to find that making babies wasn't going to be easy. Navy and I tried to get pregnant for over a year but couldn't. All those years of getting pregnant by accident, and now that I'm trying to do it on purpose, I can't. I figured it was just God's punishment for what I had done. I was a murderer, and now it was time to pay for my sins.

It was my fault that we were having trouble getting pregnant, and I needed surgery to fix it. Roughly 90 percent of my fallopian tubes were blocked by scar tissue, which was a result of my repeated abortions. I admitted to having two. Only God and I knew that there were three. Things needed cleaning up in there. Layers of scar tissue representing my past transgressions prevented anything from happening. Six months after surgery, we were pregnant, and my abortions became a distant memory.

As much as I tried, I couldn't help but blame myself. My head was constantly flooded with the *what ifs*. What if I had chosen to have those babies, and they were all alive right now? What if I hadn't have been so selfish and had faced the consequences of having those children? What if I hadn't have been so reckless? What if I hadn't have been a slut? If I had those babies, would Navy still want me? What if I had just loved myself enough?

What I did to myself was torture. I tortured myself because I thought I had deserved it. I deserved to feel these things. I deserved to swing at my head with solid wooden bats. Even though I was successfully pregnant now and on purpose, I was still being eaten alive by my guilt and the ever-sinking feeling that somehow I was undeserving of the baby I was carrying. As much as I tried to put my self-loathing behind me, I brought it with me and soon enough, my pain would rain down all over people who never covered me with a single cloud.

2019

"WHERE THE HECK HAVE YOU BEEN? ANOTHER VACA-
tion?" the guy I called Cowboy, demanded.

I plopped myself down in my chair and unpacked my bag of
books. "Yeah, but I'm back for another meeting of the asylum es-
capees." I laughed. I looked around at the other inmates, also victims of themselves, and felt I was home. It was the only place I could
be *home*. Among the like-minded is where I find my peace now.

Everyone in this place was just like me in their foundations.
They were often pissed off, annoyed, irritated, or seeking revenge
in some form. I had been doing that all along, raining down all over
people who didn't deserve it. Sometimes it was in little droplets and
other times torrential downpours that had enough power to drown
out entire relationships.

I had a habit of being like a bull in a china shop, crashing, thrashing, and breaking with each emotion that overtook me, especially anger. It was something I could not control. Its unpredictability was terrifying to me and everyone around me. I had inherited many things, but this explosive anger was by far the worst. I was ruled by emotions so strong, the only way to contain them was to kill them altogether, and that earned me the seat I was sitting in right next to Cowboy.

I've spent the last two years of my life trying to unlearn forty-something years of learned behavior. The survival skills I learned as a child were no longer serving the current me and had become extremely detrimental. Bit by bit, whatever grain of sanity that was left was disappearing. I was in a world of trouble and no longer had a way to dig myself out of it. For once in my life, I was all out of ideas. Any ideas I ever had were never good, so I sat my butt down in a room filled with other people who also had run out of ideas.

I deemed myself a head case long ago, but this had to be the apex of it. Whatever *help* I had gotten in the past didn't work. The medications, therapy, ultimatums, self-help books, writing, and sincere attempts at wanting to change never changed me. I only seemed to get progressively worse. My last resort was to be among my own. I had a huge mess to clean up, and I knew that I was the only one capable of scrubbing away the dirt.

Thirty-Three

DECEMBER 1999

BEFORE THE BABIES, WE GOT MARRIED. NAVY AND I didn't tell a soul in either of our families out of fear of what their reactions would be. We stood in front of the county judge and sealed the deal. We figured we'd just tell everyone after the fact. There was no need to bring family into it and ruin our day.

The first phone call I made was to the only one I knew would be happy and supportive. Grandma had always been my source of light, sense of safety, trust, and unwavering acceptance. My Grandma. She answered the phone on the first ring, which meant only one thing: Grandma was sitting in her cornflower-blue Ethan Allen rocker-recliner doing her morning crossword.

"Hey, Gram! Great news!" I exploded into the receiver.

"Oh yeah, kid?" Grandma always called me a kid right up until the day she died.

"Navy and I got married this morning." I could almost see her face beaming through the phone.

"Oh, that is wonderful. What did Mom and Dad say?" Ha, I hadn't told them shit because I already knew how they'd react. "Just so you know," Grandma continued, "I support you no matter what anyone says." I hung up the phone happy but with a bad taste lingering in my mouth. I knew I had to tell my parents. Bile gurgled in my stomach.

Navy and I didn't have enough money to keep the heat on, no less go on a honeymoon. We'd switch on the old Honeywell heater after getting out of the shower, stand in front of it naked until we warmed up, get dressed, and shut it back off again. Our gas bill was only around thirty bucks a month, but even that was hard to meet.

In those early days, we slept with a lot of blankets and wore layers. Some mornings our breath was visible, rising out of our mouths in crystalized steamy plumes. Northwestern Pennsylvania winters were long, gray, snowy, and breathtakingly frigid. The best we could do for ourselves was bundle up like Eskimos and fantasize about being on a hot and sunny sandy beach somewhere other than here. But we were together, and we were happy.

I did end up calling my parents about a week after Navy and I got hitched. Again, I was grateful that Mom answered and not Dad. After the usual exchange of cardboard cutout pleasantries had passed, my mother blurted out, "Let me guess. You're married. Congratulations." The phone went silent. She had hung up.

Thirty-Four

NOVEMBER 2017

THE FIRST DAY OF THE REST OF MY LIFE. NOT THIS again. I sat in my car with my head in my hands, silently praying a handful of foxhole prayers to the invisible force I was told exists. How had it come to this? My life was now at the absolute lowest of the low. I was at the bottom of the heap, the end of the line.

What a freaking embarrassment. How did this happen? What's everyone going to think? I have failed. God, if you're out there, please have mercy and save me. If you save me now, I swear I'll never fuck up again.

I only prayed when I was in trouble, as if the God I didn't believe in would answer me and help a lady out for once. Why would he, though, when all I did was screw up all the time? I only called on him when I needed to say I was sorry. I never asked the guy for anything except to rescue my ass from my stupidity.

Besides, I hated the guy. He never fucking answered me no matter how much I pleaded. The God I knew only punished me, and now I am here sitting in my car in an alley parked outside an unmarked building, shaking and sweaty. My body was in full-blown detox. I finally worked up the nerve to open the five-thousand-pound door I had been staring at and walked in. What I saw, I could not understand.

Everyone was smiling and laughing. Why in the name of holy hell are these people so damn happy? What could be so funny that these folks are busting their guts in laughter? What's so amusing about misery? I was angry, and these clowns were making me more furious. I sat my sad, detoxing, sweaty, sore ass on the faded 1970s floral print couch and looked at my feet. I was crying and full of shame.

Earlier in the day, I had been begging Navy not to leave me. I just couldn't do this life thing alone. I didn't know how. I couldn't do anything alone aside from fucking up my life and every other life within arm's distance. Everything I had touched in the last few years had magically turned to shit, and here I was dumbfounded as to how, or why, it happened.

Navy sat down next to me on the ratty old couch and stared blankly ahead. He didn't care one bit that I was sitting there a blubbering mess. I created my misery, and he had no sympathy whatsoever. I was nothing more than the drunk in his life, and he had had enough of my bullshit.

This place had to fix me because it was the end of the line. Get sober or lose everything.

Thirty-Five

2001

MOST OF THE TIME, PEOPLE DON'T REALIZE THE FULL consequences of the choices they make. For me, I just couldn't see down the road. I lived my life in tunnel vision, only caring about what was right in front of me. I never heeded warnings, refused to listen, and did whatever the hell I wanted. I only ever figured that things would just get taken care of, and I'd move on to the next thing. I made messes everywhere I went and left others to sift through the wreckage.

Navy and I were having a baby girl. I could now officially forget about all the other casualties of my wars. Still strewn about the battlefield was the wreckage, but I had once again come out on top. While soldiers still lay broken and dying, I was carrying on as if nothing had ever happened. I was going to have a baby.

I dreamed of the little girl I would soon be holding. I was going to dress her in all the pretty girly clothes that I could find. I couldn't wait to lay her down into her beautiful crib and stare in wonder, take her for long walks in the park, and teach her everything I knew about being a girl in this world. I dreamed that my mother would also dote on her and treat her like a little princess. Her Grandma would spoil her and grant her every wish, dream, and demand.

On our way back from the ultrasound, I could hardly contain my excitement. I made Navy stop at a gas station so I could use a payphone and call my mom. I couldn't wait for the twenty-minute drive home to tell her. I wanted my mom to be as happy as I was, but as soon as I dropped thirty-five cents into the slot, I wished I hadn't stopped to tell my mom anything. The voice on the other end said, "Congratulations. You just ruined your life." The line went dead and so did another piece of my heart.

Any happiness I had fell away and was replaced with intense anger. I fumed the rest of the drive home. Why couldn't my mother ever be happy for me? It seemed as if it was just impossible for her to be happy about anything. If she couldn't be happy that her daughter is having a daughter then there was nothing more I could do that would make her happy—or proud. In my mom's eyes, I once again felt as if I was somehow wrong. I had gotten pregnant, and I was having a girl, but apparently that meant I was screwing up my life again.

Instead of going to bed that night with a smile on my face and feeling joy for the future, I cried myself to sleep. Leave it to Mom to ruin what was, at that moment, the happiest moment of my life. The only conclusion I came to as I flipped my mother's words around in my head was that I had ruined her life.

Thirty-Six
2019

IT TOOK ME YEARS TO FIGURE OUT THAT IT WASN'T right. I didn't ruin my mother's life, but I had spent almost all of my life living in a giant work of fiction. The slate of my life was full of entries that were written by other people. The only entries I wrote were just words and summaries that had gotten stuck on repeat in my head. They were all the negative thoughts, opinions, and perceptions of everyone but me.

My reality didn't exist. What other people perceive is what I believed to be accurate. The book of my life had been written by everyone but me. Every page I turned had an opinion of me that I believed. I tucked each inside my head and heart where they slowly ate away at my soul. I carried words and labels with me everywhere I went. I lived them, breathed them, and became them. Chapter after chapter, I was just another version of someone else's vision.

A brain like mine cannot forget. I'm sure most people would be happy about having that ability, but quite frankly, it pisses me off. I've got a brain that never shuts off. I am convinced that when God was building me, he forgot to install my on/off switch, and if I did have one, it was broken. I'm either all on every second of the day or I'm all off, like an unplugged computer. There is no in-between setting.

Isn't it great that I can remember birthdays right down to fifth cousins twice removed, first dates, what Jess wore to my Christmas party five years ago, and the color my nails were painted on the first day of kindergarten. A brain like mine makes for a very successful person. I'm an overachiever, a leader, a visionary, a trendsetter, detailed, task oriented, self-driven, and a perfectionist. It's all because I cannot stand sitting still.

Sitting still means I would be alone in my thoughts, and therein lies the danger. I'm outnumbered up there. When I'm alone in my head, I convince myself I'm a failure, not good enough, and I could do better, be better, act better, do more, and be more. The committee in my head is always at war. I'm just a body ruled by the sum of someone else's moving parts still being crushed under the weight of a thousand second-grade teachers telling me I'll never be more than average.

So I sit on this ratty old coffee-stained couch and cry my eyes out, hoping someone around me understands, because if they don't, there truly is no hope for me.

Thirty-Seven

2002

MY POOR MOM. I'M BEING HARD ON HER, AND I HATE to think she'll read this and be upset because I love my mother. Mom is always trying her best with all of her broken pieces shifting around inside of her body too. She raised a family the best she could with the tools she had been given. How Mom was now was just the result of not having any glue. It was my fault for expecting her to fall head over heels when I told her I was having a baby.

When my baby was born, I saw some hope in Mom. It was just a little spark but a spark that I had never seen. There were some cracks in that marble after all. She was on the first plane out when her granddaughter came into the world two months too soon. My mother came. She was there.

Navy and I were at a loss. We had no idea what to do, how to feel, or how to talk about the three-pound baby hooked up to every beeping machine we had ever seen. We were terrified. There were so many questions that we wanted answers to that we never got. No doctor could tell us how she was doing. No doctor could tell us if she'd be ok. I guess that was doctors, just doing their jobs. Maybe they can't give hope.

We sat by her bedside, Navy, my mother, and I touching what we could of our baby. I'd stroke her paper-thin fingers and run my hand across her wispy tuft of strawberry blond hair. None of us knew what to say, so we just sat there staring at her and looked around the unit at the other sick, helpless babies and their equally distraught parents. Like the others, I couldn't even hold my baby. She laid there as helpless as a newly hatched bird.

I didn't feel like a mom. Having never been a mother before, I didn't know what being a mother was supposed to feel like, but it surely couldn't be this. Any of the joys of being a new mom that I had heard about did not exist in me. My switch was in the *off* position. I had my feelings buried somewhere I couldn't find, and once again I found myself in that dark hole of disassociation I had come to escape to when things were just too hard.

Why did it keep happening? Why was it that I kept shutting down and closing up shop whenever something traumatic happened? Something was seriously wrong with me. Day in and day out, I sat there at my daughter's bedside feeling nothing at all. I was ultimately out of touch with reality. It was as if I was both the character and the audience, watching myself play a role that I had never played before. I was a mother now, and I had no idea how to act in any scene.

Thirty-Eight

2017

I PROBABLY SHOULD HAVE LEFT HIM. I HAD NO IDEA how we'd ever recover from this. As I sat there, replaying all the events leading to me slumping over on this couch in a room full of freaks, I knew that I had already left long ago. I was gone. Checked out.

I may have never totally checked in, in the first place. We were quick to get married and naive about each other, about life, about anything. He was my escape from a bad situation. As I was sitting there with my guts in my throat, I knew that no matter where I went, no matter how many times I tried to run, no matter where I was or who I was with, I always followed me, and there was no escaping that.

There was nowhere to run anymore. Trapped in my head, I was a prisoner of my thoughts, and they were going to kill me. There had to be a way out of here, a way to repair all of this mess. Was the answer I was looking for inside these four walls? I was desperate. All those years of therapy—medication after failed medication—only offered temporary relief. Once I found treatment to be relatively ineffective and pills had left me relatively lifeless, I put both down and rediscovered my good old friend, alcohol.

That's why I was sitting on this ugly couch. My friend was an asshole. Someone tossed a couple of books at me and told me to read them. "Read. Oh, and come back tomorrow."

What the fuck, lady? Thanks, but I didn't even want to be here today. I knew I had nothing better to do with my time now. I had lost my job as a result of something I had done during a blackout, Navy hated me, and our kids were confused as to why their parents were home from their vacation three days early. I just wanted the heat off me, and I was willing to do anything to get that to happen.

I did go back the next day, and it was the same stupid bullshit. People were laughing and carrying on like they didn't have a care in the world. Coffee poured into Styrofoam cups and day-old dough-nuts picked over. It felt a little bit like church to me. People were milling about, exchanging pleasantries, thankful to be alive. Why was it that I wanted to die, and these folks didn't?

Thirty-Nine

2002

MOM HAD AN OPEN-ENDED TICKET AND WOULDN'T leave until she knew her granddaughter would be ok. Every day she made the two-hour car ride down to the preemie hospital with us. Every day she sat by her granddaughter's bedside, holding the teddy bear she had bought her. And every day, like me, she'd sit in an empty rocking chair with empty arms, unable to rock our little miracle.

It was two weeks before she came off the machines that had kept her alive. The day we all walked into the NICU and saw her lying peacefully asleep in her Isolette, we knew she'd be ok. It was as if this baby was becoming real now, and it was beginning to hit me that she was mine. We all took a collective sigh of relief, and Mom returned home a couple of days later. I didn't thank Mom for what she did. As usual, my head was stuck up my ass.

I couldn't even focus on what was right in front of me, no less be grateful for my mom's visit. Worse still, I had somehow convinced myself that my mom's visit had nothing to do with me or my daughter. My brain told me her motives were selfish ones. Mom had come out for herself. After all the bullshit, she was going to swoop in and save the day. Mom was going to show everyone how pleasant of a person she was, how great of a grandma she was, and how amazing of a mother she was to me. These are the fucked up things my brain came up with, which I'm sure were the farthest things from the truth. I was always thinking that people's motivation for doing something was self-seeking, because *I* was that way.

I should have just left it at *Mom showed up when it counted*, instead of making her visit all about me and about how I felt about it. Even with awareness, my brain continued to follow the narrative I had constructed. I have this new baby, and she's premature. I don't know what to do with a premature baby. I'm twenty-five years old, this is my first baby, and she's premature. I'm going to go home with her with nobody there to help, and she's premature. Are you sure this is *my* baby?.

I simply could not look at my baby and see the miracle I had. A baby is the most precious gift from God. This tiny human was given to me to raise. God trusted me with her, but I couldn't see that. I saw her prematurity as yet another punishment being handed down. God's revenge. All of those gifts I had foolishly squandered. God's punishment was a premature baby meant to make my life hard.

When she came home, I had no idea what to do. Babies don't come with a set of directions, and I sure could have used a set. Navy had gone back to work, and it was just my daughter and I.

I spent much of my days just looking at her and wondering what the hell to do. I went through the motions of what I thought *mothering* was. I fed her, changed her, and bathed her—feed, change, bathe, repeat—feeling like I didn't have a *motherly* bone in my body. I must have missed that bone in God's assembly line.

Forty

2017

SINCE I HAD LOST MY JOB AND NAVY COULDN'T STAND the sight of me, I retreated even further into myself and just did what I was supposed to, like a scolded child. I went back to the room of crazy happy people, still hoping for some answers, some help, some redemption. Mostly I was there because I wanted Navy and everyone else off my back. I wanted to learn how to control my drinking. If I could just manage it, everything would be fine.

I had no intention of getting sober at all. Never drink again? I scoffed at the idea. I couldn't wrap my head around not drinking again. How was that even possible, and why would anyone in their right mind actually want that for themselves? The hard reality was that deep down, I knew that I couldn't drink anymore.

The wheels of my life had not only come loose somewhere, but they were starting to fall off now. Things had been getting progressively worse, and I wasn't to blame. It was the alcohol's fault. If I could just put it down and walk away, or at least have a drink now and then, life would improve. Life would get better. Alcohol was my problem, and if I stopped drinking, my other problems would be solved.

I felt like the biggest loser on earth now. What I had done was the lowest of the low. I was a piece of trash, a worthless whore. I only made people angry with the things I said. I made people sad, disappointed, and hurt. My stupid drunken moments had not only ruined my own family but another family as well. Someone in the room came over to hug me. She could read the pain and struggle on my face. I let her hug me, but the deep-seated self-hatred coursed through me. A hug would not make me feel better. It wouldn't even take the edge off.

After I weaseled my way out of her uncomfortable grasp, I bolt-ed out the door. I knew my relief was only a glass of chardonnay away, but I would not pick up. I was determined to control this thing. How could a bottle of wine have so much power over me? It's not like I'm sitting at the kitchen table watching TV, and the bottle forces itself in my mouth. I'm the one who drinks it. If it is my choice to drink it, surely it was my choice to stop.

When I got home and dusted off the hug, I planted myself at the kitchen table only to realize that I couldn't sit still. I was fidgeting, sweating, and shaking and could hardly see straight. Eight days into sobriety, I was still detoxing. For fuck's sake, how long does this take? I wanted to crawl out of my skin as the sweat poured down my back. Instead, I tried holding onto the table. My knuckles whit-ened, and I focused on my breath. In through the nose four seconds, exhale through the mouth four seconds. In and out, in and out. I threw up on the floor.

You'd think I was withdrawing from heroin or something more dramatic than alcohol. It was the stuff you see in the movies. Sweat continued to drip down my back. I had to get up and do something. It didn't matter what that something was. I had nervous energy that needed out, so I grabbed a toothbrush and started scrubbing the kitchen floor grout. I had the entire floor cleaned in a matter of an hour or so. I sat back down at the table and put my head down on the cold wood, anxiety-ridden and afraid.

Forty-One

2007

NAVY AND I WOUND UP HAVING FOUR CHILDREN IN five years. We had been living in the picture-perfect postcard community for eight years, where the winters were so long they felt like three winters in a row, and the snowdrifts would get chest-high. Just like everyone else in our town, we hardly left the house. Usually, the only people who ventured out during those unforgiving months were the deer hunters and Zippo factory workers. It was cold, but our bed was always warm.

Navy had a stable job with a reliable company, and the windows of opportunity seemed to be flying open all around him. I was at home with the babies—two toddlers, a newborn, and our five-year-old daughter, who spent most of her time floating her Disney princesses through the air and making hamburgers out of Play-Doh.

"Mama, Mama, come play with me!" The last thing I wanted to do was play. I was so tired.

I had what I wanted. My dreams of having a loving husband and a large family came true. However, I was constantly questioning what I had done. Was this the life I truly wanted? Did I settle for this because I was too scared to do anything else otherwise? Could I have been more than just a mother? Well, it was too late. It was the life I had chosen. My life was no longer my own. Navy and I agreed that I would sacrifice my life so that our little humans would have a solid, stable, loving, well-rounded upbringing.

Every waking moment of my days was not my own, nor were my hours of loosely stitched together sleep. Both day and night belonged to my Play-Doh playing, corn dog–eating, green bean–hating little ones. As difficult as my days were, I was grateful. Not everyone had the luxury I had, as most homes have two working parents.

I knew I was blessed to have a husband who was willing to work his tail off to make that possible, even at the expense of his happiness. Our children were the most important beings on the planet. They were our entire world, and we revolved around them. But for me, motherhood was not a springtime frolic in a field full of daisies. I was in over my head in about ten feet of water, and damn if I didn't have an oxygen tank or any sort of life-saving scuba gear. It was me, swimming against the current, my little school of fish swimming behind.

Navy and I were doing our very best with what we had, which wasn't much. Luckily, we had some occasional monetary help from my father who had bought us our first home. My grandparents helped supply us with household things, and my aunt and uncle helped make many Christmases successful ones for our children

Navy and I didn't have many friends. Having a bucket full of kids tends to keep you homebound for a while. The friends we had consisted of a very young couple with no kids and an old retired couple from our church. That was that. The closest family we had was a good eight-hour drive away, and hardly anyone would make the drive across the state of Pennsylvania to visit us in the middle of nowhere. My uncle said the only reason he ever came out there was out of pure love. We were completely isolated. It was then, among the loneliness, exhaustion, and stress of motherhood that I had turned to alcohol to cope.

2017

ONCE I FINISHED DETOXING, I STARTED TO FEEL BET-
ter physically, but now I felt like I was alive inside a nightmare.
I was entering into reality and began grieving the life I had lost.
Gone was the promising career I had made for myself. Gone was
any amount of trust my husband had with me, and right along
with it was every last shred of dignity that remained. All of it replaced with shame.

I constantly cried and just wanted to die. There was nothing
worth living for now. I was hardly breathing down at the bottom of
the pit. I was hopeless, helpless, and afraid. Still, I had clung to the
idea that there was some magic cure out there that would help me
scrape what was left of my life back together. I needed my family
to stay intact. I needed forgiveness and someone to tell me it was
all going to be ok. Most of all, I needed to know that I was loved

because I hated myself. Yet, through my troubles and the wreckage at my feet, the desire to stop drinking just wasn't there.

Even after going through the hell of detox alone and knowing what a mess everything was, I still had no intention of quitting. Whatever I was doing to repair and appease was going to be short-lived. The plan was to stay dry until the smoke cleared from the rubble and then gradually make a triumphant return to my best friend.

There were the children, too, aware of what was happening but confused about how things wound up where they were. People just don't "lose their job" from a place they've been with for over a decade, come home from vacation early minus the friends they went with, and be on the verge of divorce. The common denominator was me. Life was completely in shambles, and I had a garage full of empty wine boxes and bottles that helped get me there.

Day after day, I returned to the room of happy people convinced that I couldn't possibly be one of them. I had heard some stories, and mine wasn't that bad, but I figured if I just stuck around for a while and faked playing their rules even for a couple more weeks, everyone in my life would see that I was at least making an effort. Besides, the haze that was in my head had begun to clear. I was sober for the first time in ten years.

I had no idea I had even been in a haze. You don't realize what a toxin is doing to your body until it's not there anymore. I was thinking more clearly, I could remember things, my headaches were gone, the shakes had tapered off, and my anxiety had begun to lessen. I was starting to feel better. It was as if someone came along and unplugged a cork in my body, draining it of the poison that had been coursing through my veins for the last eighteen years. The poison was being replaced by blood again. I felt alive.

I took the ancient text someone had gifted me weeks before out of my bag. It's spine cracked in pain as I opened it wide on my lap. After a few paragraphs, I decided this book had nothing to do with me. I closed it and left it on the table for someone it could help. I didn't want to stay sober. I wanted to learn how to stop doing so many stupid things. I wanted to learn how to stop self-sabotaging. I wanted to stop fighting with Navy. I wanted my kids to be happy. I wanted my job back. I wanted my friends back. I wanted my control back, and this book had nothing to say about any of that.

Forty-Three

2007

THE BEST WAY I COULD SUM UP MY YEARS IN Pennsylvania was with the word *lonely*. By definition, I wasn't alone by any means with the four babies I had, but I was lonely, which I would come to learn later on that alone and lonely meant two different things. I could have been in a massive crowd in an enormous city, and I still would have been lonely.

Aside from the walls in my 1950s Montgomery Ward home, there wasn't much to look at—or do. We had a neighbor next door so crazy that she had a dry erase board stuck to her front door where she left notes for people. Mostly, she'd write: Not home, come back later. Or even better: The key is under the flower pot; I'll be right back. There was a shirtless potbelly that mowed his grass every Sunday with a shotgun in his lap and a can of beer in his hand. The town's only saving grace was a small logging lake down the street where the retired came to fish at dawn every Saturday morning.

Adding to my overwhelming sense of loneliness was the ever-growing absence of Navy, who had been traveling half the summer for work. It was the four children and me full-time. The only respite I had was my pieced together sleep, and the only stress reliever and cure for my loneliness I could find was alcohol. With no friends, no family, no husband, and a sheer lack of anything to do, what else was there to help a lonely homemaker? What else would fill that feeling of despair that I had inside?

I didn't drink much. It was just enough to take the edge off and get me through the hectic days with my little ones. It was the only method of escape that I had. There was nobody to call, no one to visit, and nobody to hand a tantrum-throwing toddler to when I couldn't take it anymore. When the children were finally down for the night and the newborn was swaddled up tightly in his blanket, I'd have a simple glass of white wine to end my day. It helped me unwind and destress, and most importantly it helped me get some sleep because with the four of them and Navy gone, it seemed like the only road to peace.

I had no intention of using alcohol long-term. My family had a long history of people with drinking problems, but nobody had ever mentioned the word *alcoholic*. I had assumed my father was a functional one, and my mother seemed like she was on her way, but in my family, it was somewhat normal and perfectly acceptable.

Nobody had ever batted an eye when someone had a little too much too often. It wasn't as if it was hush-hush exactly. It was just something everyone did but was never the topic of dinner conversation. As my father said about everything else, "It is what it is," but I knew that I would never allow myself to get to the point of *it is what it is* with alcohol. I had seen the damage it caused and is still producing as it coursed through my bloodlines. I knew what it was doing to my brother and my parents, and I swore that it would never happen to me. I would be different. I would be the *normal* drinker in the family. I just needed to watch myself and keep control.

To maintain control so I didn't become one of them, I started a collection of sorts. When one bottle was empty, I'd put it in the corner of the kitchen next to the stove. When I had amassed enough to form a full set of bowling pins, I'd throw them away. It typically took a month or two to get a complete set of bowling pin wine bottles, and in the meantime, the toddlers in the house had a fun time using them as part of their constructed cities of pots and pans. For whatever reason, Navy never batted an eye over what I had been doing.

Didn't he think it strange of his wife that she was keeping a collection of empty wine bottles in the corner of the kitchen? Maybe he just assumed I was too lazy to walk outside and throw them in the trash. If it did bother him, he never once mentioned it to me, but I do admit to playing defense well before he could have ever gone on the offense. I was a manipulator after all. I knew all about smoke screens and the cover-your-ass moves from when I was a kid, and this was no different.

I was always one step ahead of Navy, or that's what I had convinced myself. If I just tell him ahead of time that wine helps me sleep better, it enhances my dinner experience, I use it to destress as a mom, it helps me relax when we go out, or it was ok because it was the weekend. I could stay ahead of any question or lurking notion he might have. I would even go as far as telling him on my third glass that it was ok, I was nothing like the rest of the family, and at that point I was. I was a typical drinker.

Sometimes I would go weeks without a glass just to prove that I could, trying to prove to myself that I was *normal*. I knew from somewhere deep inside of me, I was anything but *normal*. Without my daily destressor, I was irritable, restless, lonely, and miserable, so I continued to play my chess game to remain comfortable in my skin.

2017

I BEGAN TO WORK ON MYSELF, KNOWING THAT IT WAS halfheartedly. I had convinced myself that I was moving in the right direction no matter how slow or half-assed it was. I made sure everyone knew that I was choosing a sober life.

Look at me. Am I not amazing? Hello, world. I'm sober!

I always had an unhealthy desire to let my business be known to anyone who would listen. Look at me (waves hands), look at me! I had accomplished so much in my life that this was just going to be one more incredible, unbelievable feat tackled and dominated by the phenomenal Alexandra. I would do it because I said I would.

I counted the days of my sobriety like I was counting the days I was pregnant. I lived in a constant state of anticipation for the next day when I could broadcast yet another day without a drink. Staying sober wasn't nearly as hard as people had led me to believe. There was nothing to it.

Everything was going great. I was easily maintaining sobriety just because I said I would. If it was this easy, then maybe I didn't have a drinking problem after all. Perhaps I was not an alcoholic as I had once thought. Everyone around me had me thinking I was, but now I thought that maybe I wasn't. Weren't alcoholics people who couldn't stop drinking? I had stayed stopped on my willpower. Maybe real alcoholics didn't have willpower. I was a collector of accomplishments, and sobriety would just be another trophy to add to my shelf.

On that shelf was eighteen years' worth of dance trophies, academic awards, handwritten letters from famous athletes, and over a decade's worth of gold and silver medals from karate tournaments that I had amassed as an adult. Achieving sobriety was my next award. Surely it would be the easiest-to-achieve award yet. All I had to do was not drink, and so far so good. The truth was I had one eye on sobriety and the other on a drink. I was still in denial.

Roughly thirty days into not drinking, I was still clinging to the idea that I would someday soon be able to have a drink or two safely. I still wanted to drink and looked forward to having enough time in sobriety to have acquired some control skills. I didn't want to go get *trashed*. I just wanted to enjoy a glass of chardonnay with my dinner or be able to go out with the girls and let loose a little bit. I could drink like any normal person; I just needed a little bit of time to gather myself, get my shit together, get back some self-control.

The thought of a triumphant return to drinking consumed me every day. With enough time, I could declare myself just your typical person who drinks sometimes. How long do I have to wait? When would I be able to try again? As much as I wanted to drink, the desire to win and beat whatever it was I was fighting was stronger. My desire to win the battle of me versus wine was more potent than the desire to drink. I had to beat this imaginary foe. If that doesn't scream *alcoholic*, I don't know what does. It's the pinnacle of the word *obstinate*.

Forty-Five

2007

IT WAS THE BEGINNING OF OCTOBER WHEN NAVY came home from work and sat down with us for dinner. He said, "I have an opportunity to relocate out west. Would you be interested?" There was nothing I wanted more than to get away from this isolated, gray, frozen tundra town of nothingness, Pennsylvania.

We had gotten married here, had all of our children here, and had a house here. There will always be a beautiful spot in my heart for those things, I knew. Before Navy could give any details about his possible new job or what a move out west would entail, I dropped my fork and blurted out, "Yes, let's go!" It was as easy as picking out a gallon of milk from the grocery store. There was not a single scrap of hesitation in my voice.

I had very little to consider after all. We didn't have any friends aside from the Millers, and family was an eight-hour drive. The winters were long, the summers were short, and I had grown tired of driving eighty minutes round trip to shop at Walmart every few days for diapers and formula. We had outgrown our little three-bedroom house on Marvin Creek. A walk-in closet is no place for a baby to sleep.

I fantasized about how a move out west would look. At first I envisioned sprawling cattle ranches, cowboys, and snow fences. I saw our family sitting around a bonfire, roasting s'mores and telling ghost stories all night long. We'd go camping, hiking, and explore the beauty of the Rocky Mountains. Then I imagined the more *practical* thing for our family. We'd have a four-bedroom house in a picturesque, quiet neighborhood in a beautiful metropolitan city with lots to do.

The next day, Navy called to tell me the move out west was a go and that he'd be headed out there in a week or so to do some house hunting. As much as I wanted to join him, I knew it was an impossibility, given how poor we were and how horrible it would be to fly four little ones across the country. I had visions of screaming children, red faces, and annoyed airplane passengers. I was fine to stay behind to avoid the madness; besides, someone had to stay home and pack.

We were moving. I don't know how many people have packed up a house with a newborn in their arms and three peanut-butter-and-jelly-smeared toddlers running circles around them. Still, I imagined how much easier it would be to train a herd of rabid cats over packing up a house all on my own with four babies attached to my limbs. Those babies watched a lot of Noggin and Disney for the better part of two weeks. Navy had found a house, put down an offer, and, in less than two days, we had ourselves a home.

I managed to pack up a three-bedroom house in just a couple of weeks. I was never very successful in open-ended projects, but when plans had solid deadlines, I always did well. Deadlines gave me motivation, something to do that had an end goal. Deadlines meant there would be a sense of personal achievement for a job completed, and once I did it, I could stamp a *well done* on it and walk away proud. This grand feat was no exception.

With a little help from a few folks from our meek white church on the hill, we had the moving truck packed in a matter of a few hours. The next day, we were to begin our journey across the country toward our new lives.

Shortly after our long trek began, I wanted to have somewhere around twenty-seven drinks. I had the five-month-old and the five-year-old as my company for the trip. Navy had the four-year-old and the two-year-old. I thought I was getting the better end of our bargain, but after a few hours into the trip, I realized I was sorely mistaken. My daughter was bored to tears, and the baby hated being in his car seat, but any time the baby cried, she tended to him the best as her five-year-old self could. She didn't know how to tie her shoes, but she knew how to make her baby brother stop crying until she didn't. The baby cried straight across the great state of Kansas. All eight hours of flat, dry, windy, empty, ugly Kansas the baby wailed as if someone had chopped his foot off. Not only did I want a drink, but I also had visions of throwing myself from the car, clear onto the interstate, and being hit by a semi.

Several times I called Navy, who always kept one or two cars ahead of me, and held the phone to the backseat. "Do you hear this kid? He's been screaming nonstop like this for the last four hours.

I swear to God, if we don't stop somewhere soon, I'm going to lose my damn shit!" We drove four more hours because he was determined to make it across Kansas. It was our last big stretch until we made it to the state we'd soon call home.

Oh, my poor daughter. I'd yell at her, begging her to keep the baby quiet. She had just started kindergarten, and I was expecting her to take care of a screaming baby. It was just the tip of mistakes I'd make with my oldest that I would later try to make right.

We arrived at our destination with the last bit of my sanity hanging by a string. The baby was all right, my daughter was marginally all right, but I sure as hell wasn't. I wasn't ok when we left Pennsylvania, and I sure as hell wasn't ok now. Something was wrong, but I had no idea what. The first thing I did when we got to our new home was unload the kids and find the nearest liquor store. I needed relief.

Forty-Six

2017

I CONTINUED TO STAY SOBER UPON MY OWN WILL-power, oblivious and numb to the ones I had hurt. I was too busy grieving the life I had lost, fully immersed in an ocean full of self-pity and regret. If I hadn't done this, then that would have never happened. And if I had done this instead of that, I'd still have my career, and Navy and I would be just fine. But the fact was that I had done this and not that, so here I sat with the consequences of my actions.

I had been egregiously selfish. I had a great life, a great family, a beautiful home, close friends, and a job that brought me an over-abundance of joy every day. I had been a teacher, but not one of the garden variety. I taught martial arts and even more than that, helped shaped the character and minds of hundreds of children through the art. I could not wait to go to work each afternoon. My job hardly felt like work at all when I walked into the room and saw that sea of young faces light up when they saw me. I considered it my life's greatest work and my reason to be. Teaching was my passion and my truest love but I struck one match and watched as everything around me burned to the ground. Now I was standing in a pile of ashes with no breeze to blow any of it away.

I cried nonstop to Navy about my loss, grief, shame, and regret, but there was no mention at all about how much I destroyed him and our marriage. I loved to blame alcohol for all of my problems, and here I was doing it again. I tried to manipulate, gaslight, lie, make excuses, and cover my ass as much as I could. I hadn't done a damned thing. Had I not had the drinks, I wouldn't have gotten drunk, and I wouldn't be in this damned mess. Navy wasn't buying what I was selling. Not anymore. I was sober when I went outside the marriage. The alcohol only exposed it.

I held tight to the idea that maybe Navy saw it wrong that night. I was drunk. I couldn't have done that. I don't remember. Everyone knew what I had done. Everyone knew that I had a drinking problem, and *I* knew I had a drinking problem, but I was not of the alcoholic variety. Besides, whatever I didn't remember happening was behind me now. I was in recovery mode and knocking it out of the ballpark. Whatever I had destroyed could be recovered. There was hope.

Hope was promised the minute I pulled that thousand-pound door open and walked into the room of crazies. The rest of my life was waiting for me. If I stuck around, I'd have all the love in the world to get me there. I would be happy, and I would be free. But how long was that going to take?

How long would it be before I could get my friends back, and when would they forgive me? When would Navy move on and just get over it already? And, God, when could I go back to my job? It was pure insanity to have any of those thoughts. I had damaged so many things and so many relationships and most of it was well beyond repair. A simple "I'm sorry" meant nothing to anyone. What I had done was far beyond anything two words could fix. I clung to the thought that it would all be ok. People just needed some time to forget. I wanted this grief and guilt gone. How long did I have to suffer?

I figured that if I could just manage to do everything right from now on and stop fucking everything up, the spotlight shining on me would turn off. If I made an effort to stick around the room and listen, there'd be substantial evidence that I was committed to making changes. Don't you see what I'm doing? I'm trying to fix this shit. But I wasn't trying to fix anything. I just wanted to be left alone, and as much as I told everyone that I wasn't going to drink again, nobody was yet convinced of that—not even me.

I had already been planning my next drink. I was seeing a therapist, and I successfully manipulated her, too, but suggested my drinking had picked up because I was dealing with the stress and guilt of my actions. The poor woman never ran into my breed of human before, and if she did, she didn't have very many clients like me. I knew that within three sessions with her, I could make her believe anything that I was saying. After I manipulated our sessions, I'd then come back home with all of these new revelations about myself. I went on and on about why I did what I did. The biggest reveal of all was that I wasn't an alcoholic at all.

Drinking was just a tool to deal with my garbage. Now that all that garbage was out on the street, my coping mechanism would leave when the guilt left.

Forty-Seven

2011

THE CHANGE IN GEOGRAPHY GOT ME OUT OF ISOLA-
tion for the most part. Any isolating I was doing was now entirely
of my own doing. We moved into suburbia and quickly became immersed in everything suburbia. My neighbors had introduced me to
a couple of families just like mine, who had lives just like mine, and I
instantly hit it off with them. At last I had some friends after having
been relatively on my own for the previous decade. As a housewife
and a young mother, I craved socialization, friendships, and *me time*.

I joined groups and hung out and talked to other moms at the el-
ementary school. I organized playdates, volunteered in classrooms,
got the kids involved in activities, and had a little part-time job at
the school, supervising lunch and recess to keep me busy when I
wasn't tending to the children. Navy was no longer traveling for
work, and life was picture perfect. Only it wasn't. With all of these

things going on, I still felt empty. How could I have filled every little crumb of my life with activity and still feel empty? It didn't make sense.

I flipped back through the pages in the book of my years and read about the feeling of something always missing, but I was never sure what. One thing was consistently the same: I always filled that something-is-missing feeling with whatever felt good at the time. It had been boys, friends, church, volunteering, work, dancing, writing, working out, and generally being everyone's someone. I couldn't stand sitting still, and living in suburbia was no different. Unlike rural Pennsylvania, I had plenty to do now. Every minute of the day felt like *go time*, and when my head hit the pillow every night, I was excited to do more *stuff* tomorrow.

While friends and family watched me move at light speed, they wondered how I managed it all, while I wondered how I could do more. I wanted more friends, more activities, more get-togethers, more parties, more goals, more attention, more approval, and more accomplishments. I wanted good food at fancier restaurants, a cleaner house, happier kids, better clothes, and fancier cars. My adult life had become a competition of more, and now that I was meshed in with the middle-upper class of white yoga-pants-wearing, latte-sipping, Lexus-driving trophy wives, I found myself wanting to keep up, fit in, and be more than what they were.

My poor kids had *that* mom. I was just another mom on the block who came a dime a dozen. But even better, I would outdo everything I saw other moms doing. Someone would bring store-bought cupcakes to their child's classroom for a birthday, and I'd spend two days baking and decorating themed cupcakes for my kid's birthday. While other moms bought things for culture day, classroom holiday parties, Thanksgiving feasts, and feed-the-teachers nights, I'd spend days in my kitchen, preparing meals from scratch. I volunteered for everything, even if it was just to stuff folders on Fridays. I not only wanted to be liked, but I wanted to be noticed, appreciated, and recognized.

Little did I realize the opposite was happening. I wasn't well-versed in middle upper class white suburbia, and apparently, no mom took very well to being one-upped by another mom. How was I supposed to know? I came from rural Pennsylvania, where deer carcasses hung high from trees on front lawns to drain their blood for processing. Now I'm arguing over gluten-free desserts and the type of coffee cups Starbucks uses for the holidays. I was just trying to fit in but soon enough, the rumors about how much I liked to party began to float between bright and beaming bleached teeth mouths. I quit my job at the school and sat alone in my car until the bell rang for the next several years.

Forty-Eight

2017

I WAS GETTING BY ON DOING WHAT I WAS TOLD, AND little by little the spotlight on me had begun to fade. I had been doing what I had set out to do. I was staying sober. I hadn't had a drop in forty-seven days. Chalk this up to yet another one of my fantastic skill sets. My new superpower now was staying sober. Now with the time I had successfully collected in sobriety, could we all just move on? Hadn't I suffered enough?

I now had a friend who I talked to daily. She gave me advice, and I took it because we both knew that what I had been doing was no longer working for me. I was doing a lot of praying, reflecting, and making an effort to take responsibility for the mess that my life was. It wasn't the alcohol that had destroyed my life. It was me who destroyed my life. I could accept that. What I could not accept was that I had no control over anything. I was still managing just fine.

Not for one second did I believe I lacked power over my own life. I was running it pretty well up until recently when the wheels started falling off. I achieved so much, done so much, and rocked the shit out of it all. My ducks were all in a row, neat and tidy. It was avoidance. I filled my life with perfectionism and stayed busy, so I didn't have to sit still, acknowledge, or address what was truly going on inside of me. My life was a mess, but if I just kept busy, I wouldn't have to feel any of it.

I didn't want to be left alone in my head. It was crowded up there. It was a scary, dark place that I knew very well and tried to avoid at all costs. When I was alone in my head, I was persistently turning thoughts, ideas, words, actions, and inactions into my unique brand of reality. I couldn't tell what was real and what wasn't. I constantly wondered if people did things or said something about me on purpose, thinking they were harming me emotionally because of what I did or didn't do. I tormented myself with scenarios I played in my head, concluding that ultimately the entire world must be against me.

Busy minds need to keep working. Meanwhile, everyone around me had been growing tired of my constant maneuvering and manipulation, but doing that gave me a sense of power over what I had no control over and kept me out of my head. When I was in charge, things got done yesterday, but now I had friends trying desperately to get me out of myself and out into the world again.

"You've had a decent drying out time, haven't you? When will you be ready to go out with us again?" My friend Marie pressed. "Have you regained control? For sure, you have control over your own body," she continued. "Isn't life boring now that you aren't drinking? What do you do to fill all that time?"

Her questions seemed valid to me. What had I been doing, and was I ready to get back out there? Marie was right. I did have control over my own body. That was probably the one thing in my life that I had any control over. I learned long ago that I could do whatever I wanted with my body. Recently, I had been mindful of the food I was putting into it. I was exercising, taking care of my skin, and drinking plenty of water. I had a good handle on my body just as I always had. I told Marie I wasn't entirely sure about going out for drinks just yet. I needed a little bit more time and distance between me and the bar.

It wasn't because I wasn't perfectly capable of drinking like a normal human being, but because things at home were still unmanageable, I didn't want to cause any further turmoil. Navy and I hadn't addressed anything going on in our marriage, how it came to be in shambles, or any of the mess lying at our feet. All we had been doing was grabbing the broom and dustpan and sweeping it all up into the corner of the room to pick up later. There was still that glaring line of dirt left behind, but I picked up the rug, pushed it under, and went about my life.

Forty-Nine

2011

I AM A PERSON OF EXTREMES. I'M EITHER ALL ON OR all off, and that was the way I handled my kids as well. While I was trying to find my space in the world, I was busy trying to find theirs as well. I stepped in everywhere as that dreaded *helicopter parent* with my finger on the control button. I was the great dictator of their young lives. If I couldn't fit in with anyone, hopefully they could find their way, a place to hang their hats and feel proud.

Any *good* mom would do what I was doing. I let my kids explore every nook and cranny and take up anything and everything they showed interest in. While I wanted to give my kids the best life I possibly could, my own separate set of motives were in play.

Do you see just how incredible these kids are? Look at what they are doing now. Look at me, sacrificing all of my time for them. Aren't I a great mother?

I had a clear vision for what I wanted my kid's lives to look like, and since we were living in suburbia, I had the opportunity to give it to them. Soon I had a piano and clarinet player who danced ballet, a soccer- and saxophone-playing guitarist, an additional soccer-playing drummer, the fourth child in an expensive private preschool, and all four of them in martial arts. It was nothing short of the best for all of them, even if they were overscheduled, tired, and grumpy. Navy wasn't happy as I had scheduled us right into the poorhouse.

I had friends and family questioning what the hell I was doing and to what end. I wanted my kids to have experiences of course. I wanted to give them what Navy and I didn't have as kids, and I was doing a great job delivering on that so far. We had decided before we even had kids that I'd stay at home with them, so what else did I have to do aside from putting all of my energy into making sure they had a good life? I was kicking ass at motherhood. It was the four kids and me against the world. Moving everyone at a million miles an hour through my agenda would come at a cost far higher than any dollar bill I put into piano lessons ever would.

2018

I HAD MADE IT THROUGH THE WORST OF THE WORST.
Things were coming back together now. My drinking was under
control, and Navy and I were on the mend. After about forty-five
days of sobriety, we decided to take a little celebratory trip together
in the hopes that our still-smoldering embers would burst back into
the flames we had years earlier.

It was then, at dinner, at the most romantic spot we could find in
Estes Park, that I would convince myself and Navy that it would be
ok to have a single glass of wine. There were plenty of people back
at home who were rooting for me, and I knew it, but forget them. I
was on a rare weekend away with my husband, and we were going to
enjoy ourselves. I made a batch of hollow promises to my newfound
friends before I left. They knew I would drink again.

As my glass of wine arrived at the table, I stared at it as saliva built up in my mouth, not wanting to seem too eager to drink it. I would save it for my meal; Navy would have no suspicions otherwise. I could be a normal drinker, and I had to convince him of that. He noticed my mix of pleasure and hesitation and asked if I was ok. "Yes, I'm wonderful. I will have this glass and only this glass." The truth was that I knew I was screwing myself. One sip of that wine and my brain lit up like Times Square. We toasted to our renewed marriage and left the restaurant hopeful and grateful for our new start. I left regretting having had that drink because I instantly wanted more. I was fucked.

It was the beginning of January in the Rocky Mountains, so we had decided to stay in our room for the day. Snowmobiles weaved themselves through heavy blankets of snow, and red-plaid scarf-covered faces walked along the frozen-over lake just outside our porch door. Inside, our room was cozy, complete with a wood-burning stove and a pile of thick goose down comforters. As I watched the fire burn, a brilliant idea came to mind, and I proposed it to Navy. "So, considering that I was totally fine at dinner last night with my singular glass of wine, do you think it would be ok to go get a bottle for tonight?"

Navy looked at me and shrugged. "Well, I don't see why not if you think you have this thing under control." Yes, of course, it was under control. Everything was always under control. My mind raced. I was going to get away with it.

We both got bottles—red for him and white for me. I promised my bottle would last the weekend. If I could manage that, then for sure he'd know things would be fine. I proudly poured a glass for myself. "One glass tonight, maybe two, and that will be it for me." One or two tonight followed by one or two tomorrow, and the bottle will be gone, and I could declare success. If I could drink just this one bottle for two days, it would be proof positive that I'm not an alcoholic.

Much like everything else I had set out to do, I succeeded. Never mind the few sips I took from his bottle when mine was empty. That was just a minor detail. I went home and told my success story about how I learned that I could control my drinking. It was possible. Their made-for-television stories were nothing like mine. I was normal, sane, and didn't need anyone to call me powerless over anything.

On the way home from victory, I picked up another bottle, swearing I'd save it for the weekend, and I did. I did not, however, save the bottle of Absolut Citron that had been in the basement since Christmas. Nobody but me knew it was down there. I had it hidden in the storage area at the bottom of a large blue plastic tub labeled Baby Clothes. There, buried beneath my children's most precious items, was my bottle of stashed away rainy day liquor. I brought it upstairs to the kitchen and set it out on the counter, wondering how I could drink it without anyone knowing. I grabbed a can of seltzer water from the fridge, popped it open, and poured it in a glass full of ice cubes. I measured out a shot of vodka and dumped it in. One shot of vodka in the middle of the day would go completely unnoticed.

Fifty-One

2013

THE ONLY WAY TO DEAL WITH THESE EVER-BLOOM-ing kids of mine was to stay as involved as I could. I was on top of everything, which meant being active in their classrooms, chaper-oning field trips, and judging the science fairs. I took the kids to ap-pointments, well visits, and scheduled social lives. I was doing their laundry, cooking all the meals, and shuttling them from activity to activity. And during the time they were in school, I did my best to keep busy myself.

When I wasn't a June Cleaver wannabe, I was doing my own thing, trying to figure out just who my authentic self was. I had since graduated from a local community college with a certification in law enforcement, but a hiring freeze gave me plenty enough time to figure out that police work just wasn't for me. I turned my sails in another direction and soon landed myself into a job in which I fell in love.

It was indeed a dream job. I was in the arena I knew best: teaching kids. Going to *work* each day was the highlight of my life. Little ones, older ones, tweens, teens, and preschool-aged faces lit up when they saw me. Toothless grins spread across faces that lit me up on my insides. I felt handpicked for what I was doing, and I thought that this job was my sole purpose in life. I was behind everything this place stood for and poured my heart and soul into it. I climbed the ladder rather quickly, just as I had everywhere else in my life. Not only was I head over heels in love with my job as a teacher, but I also radiated drive, motivation, integrity, loyalty, and promise. I was also drinking—a lot.

Drinking had become something I looked forward to at the end of the day. I'd put in a good six hours a day working from home, pick the kids up from school, cart them off to wherever they needed to be, or drag them with me to work where they'd eat their dinner and do their homework until their dad came to scoop them up to take them home. I'd get back around 9:00 p.m. and pour myself a giant glass of wine.

Bottles were no longer cutting it. I was making far too many trips to the liquor store and started to get worried about what the people who worked there thought of me coming in every other day. The bottles were also creating far too much trash each week, not to mention they'd clunk around in the trash bags as I hauled them out to the street. What would our neighbors think? I discovered the glory and convenience of boxed wine. It was cheap, had about twenty-five servings per box, and the neighbors would never hear me hauling boxes out to the curb. Boxed wine also fit better on my pantry shelves, and the spout was great for easy pouring. Boxed wine was a total game changer. Of course, the ease and convenience would turn this moderate drinker into a heavy one.

My pantry turned into a wine buffet. Not only was there boxed wine, but a liquor store warehouse opened up near home. Boxed wine lined the entire top shelf of the pantry. Spouts facing outward and ready to pour were selections of domestic and imported merlots, burgundies, chardonnays, blushes, and pinots.. Every few weeks, my shopping cart at the warehouse overflowed as I couldn't *not* try something new that I saw.

Ooh la la! This one is French. I have to try this French one. I love the art on this one. I might even save it because it's so pretty. I can't decide between this chardonnay and that chardonnay, so let's get both. We have company next weekend, so I better make sure there's enough for everyone. What? It's not like it's going to go bad if I buy this much.

Then there were the children who had once had an ever-present mom who was now becoming increasingly unavailable to them mentally and emotionally. I was becoming unpredictable, angry, demanding, overcritical, and explosive.

Fifty-Two

2018

MY FEEBLE ATTEMPT AT TRYING TO CONTROL MY drinking had failed miserably. After I began pouring vodka into my seltzer water, I could no longer deny that I had a problem. I was an alcoholic. Healthy people don't have to hide their drinking by stashing bottles and glasses all over the house. Normal drinkers don't need to get drunk before they socialize. Normal people don't pass out every night; normal people fall asleep. Normal people don't start thinking about when they can drink again as soon as they open their eyes in the morning.

Clearly, I was not *normal people*. Even though it was so prevalent in my family, I had no idea what alcoholism was, aside from the fact that I was yet another victim of it. I knew I would either die of this, or I would get fucking serious and get sober. I decided that I would take my chances with death, figuring that only older people or gutter drunks ever died from alcoholism, not people like me.

As bad as it was getting, I told Navy not to bother me about my drinking. I was utterly functional right up until the point I was fired from my job, which meant I was managing just fine. "I only drink because it's fun. I like the effect, and it helps me relax. It makes me feel good." So I drank, and Navy left me alone.

Oh, pity on the poor woman who wanted to help me. She could see through my lies and manipulation as nobody else could. She knew I was in immediate danger; the inevitable collapse was coming. But she, too, backed off of me when I told her, "I got it." I laughed off the suggestion of trying to control my drinking again. I was doing just fine with it, so why try to control it now? Even Navy wasn't buying the death sentence.

Game on! Those boxes of wine I had become a collector of, for their uniqueness, began turning into a pile of rubbish for the Mile High Marketplace. Too many boxes meant too much clutter, and damn if my house was going to look out of order. I had an image to maintain. I even had my closest friend fooled into believing I didn't have a problem. The same went for the kid's teachers, our neighbors, the church, and anyone else I had contact with. On the outside, it was the picture-perfect life based upon the sixteen-by-twenty canvas on the wall of the living room; my family was picture perfect too. The image I so proudly presented to the world was nothing more than one massive lie.

Navy was spiraling down the drain right along with me. He was becoming just as dead on the inside as I was. Navy tried desperately to keep up with my ever-growing insanity. And the kids? I no longer knew who they were aside from beings that floated about the house in their own confined shells, eating and drinking and yammering on about nonsense. Somewhere along the way, I had stopped paying attention. It was as if I closed my eyes for a minute and opened them to find four moody, angsty teenagers. Negativity was the smell that reeked in our house. The kids and Navy all spent their days tiptoe-ing on eggshells.

Every single day the ghosts in the household would gauge my mood and adjust themselves accordingly. They were now doing the same thing I had done as a kid. Warning: Approach with highly guarded caution or not at all. Hide when arguing or fighting erupts. I had become the very thing I hated.

Fifty-Three

2016

THERE WERE SO MANY ATTRIBUTES ABOUT MYSELF that screamed the word *alcoholic*. Homelife aside, my job had turned into so much more than I had ever anticipated. Within a year, I had climbed the ladder right to the very top. Now I was standing on the roof, looking down at all the little folks on the ground below. What's it like to be so ordinary?

The more power I got, the more power I sought. I was increasingly trying to control every aspect of my life. It was a shell game of organizing, shuffling, and reorganizing chunks of my life. I would put my hand on a shell and shift it around when nobody was looking. I hoped my game would fool everyone into thinking I had my life managed. See this? Now you don't. I put in long days at home and continued to work every evening, not caring or scarcely thinking about my family at all. I was determined to manage, so no surprise to anyone that I had become one.

The more I got involved at work, the less I paid attention to my homelife, thinking that the kids were getting older and things would take care of themselves for the most part. I took it upon my-self to decide that Navy was the better option for our kids instead of me. He could talk to them about anything. I, on the other hand, didn't know how.

I hadn't taken the time to learn how to talk to the kids. I only knew one way, and that was my way. I had the attitude of "Well, if you're not going to listen to me, then I can't help you." And for the most part, that was true. My kids frustrated me, and I had little to no patience for excuses. Simple things made me angry, and hard things got punted over to the more rational parent. It made sense to me. Rather than learn how to parent instead of randomly firing off the cuff at something I deemed as nonsense, "Go talk to your dad" had become my smoother, softer way, and it protected my kids from my unpredictable moods.

I deemed myself completely unequipped for *real* parenting. I just wasn't capable of having serious conversations, handing down severe punishments, or comforting any of them when they need-ed it. I could, however, throw them one heck of a birthday party, and they could count on me for being there for every single school event, concert, game, or performance. I simply had no idea how to parent, but for some reason, Navy did. Instead of being grateful, I was jealous that he knew how to talk to the kids and I didn't. The truth was that I just didn't put in the effort with any of them and was riddled with guilt that I wasn't the mother of storybooks.

Somewhere along my journey in motherhood, I had completely detached. I was so immersed in my sense of self and inflated importance that I didn't even know who my kids truly were as people. The only thing my kids came to count on from me was emotional distance and yelling when things weren't up to my expectations. I had expected nothing short of the best from all of them. Meanwhile, my eldest child's mental health was in steady decline.

She had become isolated, moody, and withdrawn. Red flags were sprouting up all over the place, and I had either failed to see them or flat out ignored them, chalking it up to being a teenager. I had been moody and distant at that age too. I looked to Navy to help me with her because I had no idea what to do.

Navy took care of everything because he had to. My only set of eyes were focused inward. Rather than address what was happening with my daughter, I was just pissed that there was an issue. She had everything, so I failed to understand why she was so upset. What was so bad about her life that she was feeling the way she was? Why was she making such a big deal out of everything? Why couldn't she just suck it up, fix it, and carry on as I do? I had failed her somewhere. She was not the rough and tumble kid that I raised. I raised a strong girl capable of holding the world in her back pocket.

The school had eventually called me in to *talk*. I was expecting to hear how horrible of a mother I was. Instead, the floor fell out beneath me. It hadn't been about me at all. No wonder my daughter was such a wreck. Still, I had no idea what to do about it. She would need extensive therapy, yes, and although I should have been sympathetic, I found myself even angrier than before. I was angry that my daughter was powerless over her situation, mad that the school counselor had to tell me what to do, angry at the other kid and his mother, and angry at myself for being such a shitty mom. How could something so detrimental go unnoticed for so long? I went home and got drunk.

Fifty-Four

2018

DRINKING HAD BECOME MY ANSWER TO EVERYTHING. I always pressed people to get together for drinks, whether we played cards at my house or went to some random bar in town. If going out for drinks wasn't on the agenda, I made sure that no matter where we wound up, there would be liquor there; otherwise, I would just stay home and drink there.

I had set rules for myself to give myself the illusion that I still had control. During the week, I wouldn't drink before 4:00 p.m. If it were a weekend, I wouldn't drink before noon, unless we were on vacation or out to breakfast because then it was completely acceptable to have a mimosa or two to fit in with everyone else. I would only drink wine and not the hard stuff, unless of course I was out of wine. Then I'd drink whatever was in the house, but the hard stuff had to be colorless so nobody would notice I was drinking it. All of these rules seemed perfectly acceptable to me.

I'd drink when I had a bad day, or if it was a good day. If someone got me mad, I'd drink. If someone made me happy, I'd drink. If something good happened to a friend or family member, then it was cause for celebration. I'd drink. If someone were sick, I'd drink. If I couldn't sleep, I'd drink. I'd drink because I slept well. If we went camping, hiking, or boating, I drank. If there was a function at the kid's school, a game, or an event, I drank. I drank over everything and nothing at all. My entire life revolved around my drinking, thoughts of drinking, and hangover management. I drank every single day, and I drank to get drunk. The fun that I once had with having a few were long gone. I needed to drink now, or I was sick. And when I did get drunk, I was sick. Either way, I was sick, but I'd rather be sick with it than sick and suffering without it. Without it, I couldn't function.

Most of my drinking was at night. My family would gather up to eat dinner, and I would sit there drinking mine. I knew if I ate something, it would pass right through me in a matter of minutes. I hardly ate anything at all anymore because I knew I would just get sick. By the time bedtime rolled around, I would have justified at least four or five goblets full of wine.

Every night, I'd tell myself that I could have a couple because I no longer had a job to go to. After two glasses, I'd then tell myself it was ok to have more because I didn't have to wake up until 7:00 a.m. to take the kids to school. I decided that if I had four glasses of wine, I could just go back to bed after I dropped them off, and then I'd stop justifying drinks and have five, because who cares anymore?

I knew every night that I'd wake up with a miserable hangover, but it would be all right. I could tolerate it by throwing down a bunch of pills and drinking a quart of Gatorade. I'd sleep it off all morning and wake up at noon to half of my day wasted. Even at noon, I would not feel better until I could drink again. I was obsessed, and there was no shutting it off.

I canceled plans with friends and was a no-show at events and parties. For coffee dates and lunch plans, I always had a last-minute excuse as to why I couldn't go. It wasn't because these places didn't have alcohol. It was because I was ashamed. I was better off drinking alone than to expose anyone to my horrible secret. I didn't want anyone to know how bad I had gotten, how far into the gutter I had fallen. Worst of all was the fact that my family was miserable and I was too drunk to care. My marriage collapsed beneath the weight of my selfishness, and I didn't care about that either. I told myself that if Navy left, it would make no difference to me. I had checked out on him years ago, and I had wondered if I had ever really checked in.

No matter what I tried, I couldn't connect with either Navy or our children. Emotionally, I was like a ten-year-old, even though the calendar read forty-two. I blamed everyone but myself for what was falling apart, even though I knew it was me who was causing all the trouble. I was just so very sad and had a hurt that ran so deeply within me that now that pain was leaking out all over everyone else. And then I found out that Mom was dying from alcoholism. Life was quickly becoming too much to bear.

Fifty-Five

2017

WE WERE ON VACATION WHEN I LOST MY JOB AND MY life ended, as I knew it. It felt as if someone very close to me had died. My body was pumped through with bullet holes; guilt and shame leaked like blood. I had nobody to point the finger at but me, yet I still could not look at myself in the mirror and accept the blame.

I expected everyone to feel sorry for me. I lost the only job I had ever loved. That job was my calling, my life's passion, and nobody seemed to give a damn about that loss but me. I had utterly destroyed my marriage, my friends turned their backs to me, and I still could not accept the truth. I sat down next to Butterscotch and sniffled my way through my sad story. A room full of faces wearing genuine empathy nodded concern and understanding in my direction. They had destroyed their lives too. I wasn't alone, and if I stuck around, I would never be alone again.

Fifty-Six

SUMMER, 2018

I SAT AT MY PARENTS' KITCHEN TABLE AND WAITED for them to get back from the doctor's office. They had no idea that I was coming. I hopped on a plane, rented myself a car, and let myself in through the garage door. Surprise! I'm here for a visit. What I came for was some answers, and I wasn't leaving until I knew what the hell was going on with Mom.

I heard the garage door open just as I was finishing off my mom's morning crossword by filling it in with a bunch of random letters. In came my dad, holding the door for my mother, who was following slowly after with her walker. Mom had fallen so many times and had broken so many bones that she could no longer walk without help, not to mention the neuropathy that took sensation out of her legs.

I was shocked by what I saw when Mom walked in. She looked like she had aged ten years within the last two. Mom was barely recognizable.

"What the hell are you doing here?" she asked. Not exactly the hello I was looking for, but it was Mom after all.

"Thought I'd come for a quick visit to see how you're doing, and it doesn't look like it's too good right now." Silence.

I called Navy that night as I was lying on my old bed in my old room, staring up at the thirty-year-old frozen-in-time photos of me as a ballerina. "They won't tell me anything. I can't believe I dropped everything to come out here, and they won't say a damn thing." I was livid. All I got out of them was "Mom is fine, and everything is ok." My brain started to turn all around. I bet she doesn't even want me here. She sounded almost disappointed or mad when she walked in and saw me there. I'm probably invading her space, threw a wrench in her plans, and now I'm just in the way of that.

When Mom and Dad left for yet another doctor's appointment the next morning, I went sleuthing around. I didn't have to look hard. Right there next to the thirteen-inch TV in the kitchen was a stack of papers. A couple of pages down and I found exactly what I was looking for: mom's medical record.

She was sicker than I had anticipated. And by the looks of her laundry list of ailments, I was guessing she had five years left, at best, and I thought even that was being generous. Between what I saw yesterday when I got here and what I just read today, I couldn't imagine her having two more years on this earth. Mom was dying from alcoholism. I decided I would confront them at dinner. Someone had to take control of this. Something had to change. I would demand it.

"Ma, I found your health history. Why didn't you tell me you had so many problems? You need help, and Dad can't do it all. I want you to sell the house and come live near me." Mom wouldn't even look at me. She stared out the window, intently watching a squirrel try to climb his way up an oiled post to reach birdseed. She refused to listen to anything I was saying. Dad agreed with me, but Mom would have none of it. After about ten more minutes of pressing, Mom finally spoke up.

She continued staring out of the bay window in the kitchen overlooking the swimming pool. She crossed her arms and said, "No, I am not going anywhere."

It felt like I was talking to a four-year-old who was on the verge of a meltdown. I got up from the table and went up to my old bedroom to pack my things. I would leave in the morning, defeated and feeling just as helpless as I did in Sunday school.

After I had packed my stuff, I went straight to the liquor store. I had stayed sober that weekend so I could be in the right state of mind for a serious conversation with my parents. But what was the point now? Mom had given up on life and chained Dad up with her. That night, Dad and I sat in the garage, and I drank 1.5 liters of wine. I had honestly given up. The day's saving grace was when my dad apologized there, in that garage that night. With his eyes staring into the glow of the New York Yankees up at bat came the most unexpected sentence I had ever heard out of my father: "I'm sorry for everything that happened to you when you were a kid."

PART III

Fifty-Seven

LAST CALL

WHEN I RELAPSED, I RELAPSED HARD. THE LAST NINE months had been one alcohol-induced haze, with each hangover worse than the next. My entire life had turned into one massive shit show, and worst of all, I had ceased caring about anything but my next drink.

I couldn't say I blamed Navy when he took off for a weekend in Vegas with his friends, leaving me here swimming around in my abyss of wine. I was now passing out drunk every night and waking up still drunk in the morning. I pieced together enough hours during the day until the clock told me an acceptable time to drink again. The kids were an afterthought, if I had even given them a thought at all. I spent most of my time up in my bedroom, drunk and shut out from the rest of the world. It was my life now, and I knew if I kept it up, I would be dead in no time.

Day after miserable day, I had concluded that maybe I was meant to die this way. I had reached a level of self-loathing I didn't know existed. I never hated anyone more than I hated myself. Maybe after all of the bullshit I had put everyone through, I was deserving of an alcoholic death, so I began a nightly prayer for it.

God, please make tonight the night I drink myself to death. God, have mercy on everyone around me, and please just take me.

Of course, there was no such luck. I'd always wake up the next morning angry that I did. God never listens.

The night before Navy returned from his trip, I thought about the 9 mm that I had locked up in our biometric safe. I kept the Glock 17 loaded with a bullet in the chamber, cocked and ready for any intruder that might come in the middle of the night. The thoughts churned once again inside my crowded head, and they were making a horrible noise.

Shut up! Shut up in there.

I wasn't waiting for an intruder to kill me. I already had one. It snuck in under the guise of a good time. It promised me things, and I believed it. Things would be better if…the pain would go away, if…you could deal with everything, if…you just had a couple of glasses of wine.

Let me in, and I promise not to rob you. I swear!

I took the gun out of the safe and held it in my hand. I clicked off the safety, sat on the edge of the bed, and asked the God I had come to hate for forgiveness. Just as I tasted the cold steel of the barrel, there was a gentle little knock at the door. It was my youngest boy asking if he could come in and sleep on his dad's side of the bed for the night. In a panic, I scrambled for the safe, beep-click-beep. My trembling, sweaty hands placed the gun ever so gently back in the safe, and then I opened the door for my son. He hugged me good night and crawled into bed, and I cried myself to sleep with one of his hands resting softly on my arm.

I woke up with such an eerie feeling. Mixed in with my God-awful hangover and feelings of guilt and shame from what had nearly happened the night before, looming gray clouds hung thick overhead. Navy had ignored the majority of my phone calls and text messages while he was away, and I spent my day unsettled and anxious over the reasons why.

He got back home from his Vegas rendezvous just as the kids and I were sitting down for dinner. As usual, I was at the table with my goblet of chardonnay, drinking my dinner. I looked up at my family proudly, trying to change the temperature of the air. "Hey! Guess who's judging the middle school science fair this year?" Look at me! Mother of the year. I always maintained this façade, even in the face of my life completely falling apart. Something had to show the world that I was still somewhat together and managing quite fine.

The kids and Navy were unimpressed. Nobody cared. They had also arrived at the point of not caring anymore. It was one thing to destroy myself, another to see everyone else around me being pulled right down into the same pit. Everyone just ate their food and disappeared from the table as quickly as they came.

Navy had an announcement, too, but it was for my ears only. "Let's go for a walk." His voice was cold. My stomach dropped.

We got about halfway down the street when he told me he want-ed a divorce. I was drinking for so long I had lost the ability to feel. So when he broke the news, I didn't feel anything at all. It had gotten so bad that by this point, I'm sure if someone stabbed me to death in the middle of that street, I probably wouldn't have felt that either.

I fell to my knees in a defeated heap and buried my face in my hands, not from hurt but from something else I couldn't identify. Last night I had a loaded gun in my mouth, and today a nineteen-year marriage was ending. Yet, the tears would not come. I even tried to cry, but the tears would not come. I was completely void of all emotion. How could the last two days of my life, so fresh and raw, have absolutely no feeling tied to them? What kind of person loses it all and feels nothing?

I realized that night, as I sat alone in a hotel room twenty-five miles from home, just how sick I was. There was no other explanation. I was sick, and I was dying. I needed help for most of my life but never once wanted it. My *rock bottom* had a basement, and this was it. As I sat on the cold and dusty concrete floor, I looked up. There I saw the smallest beam of light, streaming in like a sunrise just cresting over the horizon. It was hope. It was still there waiting for me, and I wanted it.

What I didn't want was to go home. Check out was at 11:00 a.m., and I waited until 10:58 a.m. to turn in my key.

"Rough night?" asked the woman in the royal-blue pinstripe suit, as she peered over her Walmart readers. It was apparent I hadn't slept, and my body had once again begun to detox.

This time was far worse than the last. I handed my key over and excused myself to the bathroom, barely making it into the stall before I wretched all over the floor. Every nerve in my body shuddered and ached. I figured that if I died right there on the bathroom floor of that hotel, nobody would have cared anyway. Everything I had ever loved and cared for was gone. Various calls and texts I had made and sent the night before came up just as empty as I was.

I knew of only one place where I could go instead of home, and that was the land of crazy folks. I knew that I'd always be welcome there no matter how far down I had fallen. That room full of lunatics would be there to catch me, and they would be happy doing it. They knew me because, to them, it was just like looking in a mirror, or how a twin knows their twin. My threads were as familiar to them as their own. If you wove a tapestry of our threads into one rug, there would be no differences except at the seams.

I drove my sorry ass home and walked in to see my four kids staring at me with blank expressions as Navy was moving his belongings into the basement. I dropped my backpack down in the kitchen and walked back out without saying a word. There were no longer any words to make this better. Nothing would make this better.

I drove across town and poured myself back into the same seat I had been sitting in nine months before and sat there crying my way through the entire hour. I saw this movie before, and here it was, playing for me again. My life was up in flames from the gasoline I had poured. I had fully conceded now, admitted utter defeat. I knew my options were limited to only two: drink myself to death, or shut the fuck up and listen and survive. The choice was abundantly clear now, because I knew I couldn't run anymore. My legs had grown so tired. I wanted to stop drinking this time. I wanted to get well. The warning was that things would only get worse had I continued to drink, and now I believed it. Things had gotten worse. Navy and I were discussing the vision of our impending separate lives. How much worse could it possibly get than losing my family?

I had to change everything now, including my mind, which up until now had proven fruitless. Engraved on my slate was so many years of people doubting me, calling me a liar, and screaming in my face about not even having the ability to change and that I had no reason to try. And maybe it had been true, that I was incapable of change because I hadn't wanted to, but that itself was changing now. I had become the last willing participant. Everyone else had just been patiently waiting for the light to come on.

As I sat down this time, I was at the table. There was no more trying to blend in on the ratty old couch, bailing early, or keeping my head down. I closed my eyes to pray, and for the first time since I was a child, I opened my heart. A wave of calm washed over me as I accepted the fact that, yes, I was an alcoholic, that I had always been an alcoholic, and I had reached the point of surrender. There was only one person who could save me, and it wasn't myself. All I had done was make a mess, and the only source of strength I would find had to come from somewhere else. It had to come from God.

I came to the point of accepting things as they were, and those things I could not change. I could not change the fact that I was an alcoholic. I could not change the fact that I had hurt people, and I could not change the fact that almost everyone I knew had written me off as a lost cause. I pulled up on the emergency brake to stop my car from crashing, and I looked back to see that all of my passengers were suffering from whiplash.

Nobody was surprised to see me back. If anything, everyone was happy I was there, as most people don't make it back when they leave. They go back to drinking and either wind up in prison or they die, and I understand why they do it. Change is terrifying, especially to those who have brains like mine. My mind won't silence. The on/off switch is broken. Ego, control, and obstinance all stand in the way of getting well.

For the first time in my forty-two years, I reached out my hand and asked for help and was willing to receive it. For so long, I had demanded I do things alone simply because I thought I could. I didn't need help from anyone. I had always crossed my arms and tightened my lips to open hands.

No, I don't need your help. I got it, but thanks.

The truth was I had needed help for a very long time, and it wasn't just with drinking. I needed help way back when I was five years old and didn't get it. The rest was just a snowball of events that had me believing that I had to do it alone.

Now it was about shutting up and listening. No longer was I to rely on those old survival skills because they were obviously no longer working for me. My way of thinking had absolutely ruined my life. I had been sitting on the coattails of others, surviving off the sweat and backbones of the people who put in the hard work, only to swoop in and scoop up all the credit because I had somehow convinced everyone that it was me who saved the day. The thought that I could manage my life, as well as everyone else's lives, had ruined me. God had to enter in, and I would have to let Him, as He was the only one who could save me now.

I had every reason to be a drunk. For decades, my thoughts plagued me.

If you lived my life, you'd drink too. If you had to go through what I went through as a kid, you'd drink too. If you were sexually abused and violated and had to survive in unpredictable violence, you'd drink too.

It was time to stop playing victim. It was time to take full accountability, and it was time to stop fucking around and pouring poison into my body to cope. It was time to quit fighting that little beam of light that had been trying to illuminate my darkness. It was time to accept God, believe in Him, and have faith. But aside from what Grandma told me, I still had no proof that God existed.

Fifty-Eight

THE CASE FOR GOD

THE FOUNDATION OF GOD WAS ALWAYS THERE. I'M not sure if I was born with it, or someone implanted the idea very early on that God exists, and that He cannot *not* exist. If He did exist and still does exist, then where the heck was He all this time? Where was the Almighty and all-powerful when all the bad shit was happening? Where was my Great Protector then? Why did He allow such awful things? I was not a God fan.

The people around me were real. The things surrounding me were real. God is not something that I can see; therefore, He can't be real. I could not, for some reason, see His presence having been anywhere. But I thought maybe He was everywhere, and it's been me who's been ignoring Him and refusing to see. I had so many things blocking me from salvation, yet something, someone, had led me back to the place I knew I'd find Him, if I just had the will to seek.

So there I sat contemplating my belly button instead of just let-ting go. The wheels in my head were turning just as they always had. The only God I knew was the one in which I sent foxhole prayers. Sometimes He answered, and sometimes I got fucked. Maybe God was there in both places. Maybe He saved me from my shit *and* caused my shit to happen, so I'd wake the heck up already. How many messages did I need before I accepted that I was horrible at running the show? Any time I took the reins of my life, I was run-ning it off into the ditch.

The ego in me was unpalatable. When situations had a favor-able outcome to me, God was good. If things didn't work out the way I wanted them to, well, God was an asshole. What if I just let go, and let the chips fall as they may? No matter what my attitude, life was going to happen regardless.

The little flicker of light I saw from the basement floor illumi-nated my dark pit just a little bit more. I was utterly powerless in my ability to control my drinking. If I didn't have power over that, how could I possibly have had dominion over anything in my life? There was no person, place, thing, or situation I could manage effectively, and maybe it was because I was trying to be both the puppet and the one pulling the strings. It was a relief to know that I didn't have to do both.

It was as simple as admitting my way was not working and ac-cept complete surrender to His will. I would move forward from here, trying to live in each moment; however, it arrived in whatever form it took. Maybe the spoon-fed nonsense all those years might have some truth to it, and giving it all to God seemed a far better idea than the alternative.

God could help me get sober, and as I began to battle the worst detox of my life, I had an overwhelming feeling that I wasn't alone. As I laid around for two weeks, consumed by hammering headaches, insomnia, nonstop nausea, and a horrible case of the shakes, something was helping me stay calm. Yes, I was suffering, but I felt blanketed in peace and understanding.

Fifty-Nine

PAPER PLATES ARE COMPLICATED

I DON'T KNOW WHY I FELT THE NEED TO TELL MY PAR-
ents about what I was doing now, but I guess the little freckled-face
girl who was still very much alive inside this adult body always
wanted Mom and Dad to be proud. It was still a constant craving
that needed feeding.

I wasn't drinking anymore, and with God's help, I would never
take another drink again. My parents didn't quite understand why
I had to go to such an extreme. I wasn't the one with a drinking
problem; that was my brother. He was the real alcoholic of the family. He had been to prison, wrecked cars, and stacked up DUIs like
tissues in a box. No, I wasn't *that bad*, they attested. Oh, but I was. I
was just as gone. My ending may be different than my brother's, but
our stories were the same. We were and are alcoholics.

Alcoholism isn't just the homeless guy drinking out of a brown paper bag or the old lady pushing the shopping cart. It's the housewives, bankers, doctors, teachers, and neighbors. People who lead seemingly *normal* lives suffer just as much as the guy sleeping on the church doorstep covered in newspaper. We may look different, but we are all the same.

I gave up trying to explain. Dad offered support in the only way he knew how. "Well, if you got your black belt, then you can do anything." My parents didn't have to understand, but the fact that they were trying to was good enough for me. Ultimately, I wasn't doing this for their love, attention, or approval. I was doing this for me. There was something there in that head of mine that had hoped they would sober up too. As I was falling off the cliff of alcoholism, I was still reaching out my hand to them, hoping they'd climb back up to the edge with me. But that was not my job. It was their weight to carry.

I couldn't give away what I didn't have, and in the few short weeks I had been sober for the second time around, I was in no position whatsoever to say a damn word to them about their sobriety, or lack thereof. It wasn't my story. It wasn't my lane. I knew that because I couldn't even save myself, there was no way I could ever save them. My parents had to come to their own conclusions about that. I just loved them and wanted to share the little bit of hope that I had found.

My brother called me a few days later. I answered the phone to a question. He asked, "How did you know?"

I paused for the right words, as it was my brother after all—the brother who was labeled the *real alcoholic*. I needed to choose my words carefully because he was still very much active in his form of the disease. "I knew when I couldn't stop, even when I wanted to. When I swore I didn't want to drink today, I drank anyway."

He said it sounded familiar. "Yeah, but you haven't done what I've done. You haven't made the mess I have. You haven't destroyed your entire life because of your drinking. You still have some shit left. You're not even close."

Even alcoholism had to be a competition. My brother insisted his level of hell was more profound than mine. As far as I knew, it could have been. I had a front-row seat to what he went through, but I wasn't interested in the one-upping and comparisons of our disease. Just because I didn't land in prison doesn't mean I wasn't in my special form of hell. I built my prison in my head, and there was no parole from those bars.

I closed my eyes every night to the same scenarios, and I'd replay them, imagining a different ending to each. My brain still wanted to change what happened, even though it was impossible. In every ending, I came out on top. I stood up for myself, I spoke up, I told people how I felt, I respected my body, I had boundaries, and I told people no. Those were my *good* nights.

Other nights I would spend complicating paper plates.

I know TJ said this, but what if he meant that? Why did so many people bail on my party two years ago? Did I do something wrong? Are they honestly my friends or just pretending to like me? Is my neighbor going to think I'm unfriendly because I didn't say hello yesterday? What about the guy I waved to last week who didn't wave back? What a rude bastard.

I must have been very important to be taking up so much space in other people's thoughts. Maybe, just maybe, people didn't think of me at all. God knows I didn't think about them much.

Liquor was the only thing that stopped the brain from spinning. I wasn't unique and sure as hell wasn't as important as my ego said I was. I had a list that ran a mile, filled with people I thought did me wrong, harmed me, or hurt me in some way. Not once was I ever willing to look at my part in any of it. I was always the victim. Who else had a brain like mine? My brother, for one, and countless others. The solution was to get out of my head. But how? My crutches were gone, and I had no idea how to walk without them.

Solutions come in many forms, and up until that room full of crazy folks, the only solution I had was drinking. Total blotting out of consciousness was my answer to everything. It made the voices stop and memories disappear. The only problem with my solution was that it was killing me. As my brain floated around in its last sip of chardonnay, I cracked open the suggested reading material once again and grabbed a pen.

Sixty

CRAWLING

THINGS AT HOME WERE A DAMNED MESS. NAVY WAS living in the basement and looking into the steps needed to proceed with our divorce. Not even as much as a word was exchanged between us in weeks. I was spending my time in a daze, much like I had when I left the mental ward eighteen years prior, and Navy was now just an awkward roommate.

I was a lifeless zombie on the couch in the living room once again. I only got up to eat and go to the bathroom. I managed to take the kids to school each day, but after returning home, it was just me and my thoughts and no coping mechanism. My head ached from hours of crying, and my body screamed for alcohol. Yet I would not listen, no matter how much my body shook, or how many tears fell from my baby-blue puffy, bloodshot eyes.

I was crawling out of my skin on the couch and felt like I was going to fall off. I moved down to the floor and felt worse. I was writhing in pain, my body twisted into ball after fetal ball, insides racked with emotional devastation. I was feeling. I watched the minutes tick by on the harmony clock hanging on the living room wall. My only source of relief was coming soon, and it did not come from a bottle but a room full of strangers.

The last thing I was expecting was applause at the mention of being a few weeks sober. Praise, as much as I had always yearned for it, made me uncomfortable. It was even worse now that I was sober. I felt embarrassed by it. I had done nothing deserving of applause. I was still dry after a few weeks, big deal. But it was a big deal to everyone around me. It was a long time between drinks. For me, it was just a bunch of excruciating twenty-four-hour days that felt more like twenty-eight hours.

I was struggling to keep holding on, and people took notice of that. I couldn't figure out how they knew, and then I remembered from the year before when I tried this thing the first time. They know I'm struggling because they, too, knew the same damned struggle. We are the same. My anxiety was through the roof to begin with, and the applause had now made it so much worse. I was going to pass out right there at the table if I didn't get some air. I bolted out the door and sat down on the curb. I closed my eyes and practiced the breathing exercises I had learned so many years ago at the hospital.

As I began to come down from my state of panic and my heart assumed its normal rhythm, I opened my eyes to see one of the guys from the room standing in front of me. "You ok, kid? Do you wanna go grab a coffee or something and talk for a little bit?" I had seen this guy a few times before, and he seemed harmless enough. But do I blindly trust this person I don't know and go with him for a coffee?

Before my brain could start flipping around like dice, I quickly decided I'd go. "Sure, but I think if I pour caffeine into this anxiety, I might have a heart attack." I laughed nervously.

"Please don't worry. I'm not out to sleep with you or anything like that. I want to help."

I had never trusted a single man in my entire life, not even Navy. I'm not sure what it was about this guy from the room, but keeping in mind that everything I had ever done was wrong, I let my guard down a little bit. We met for coffee every day for the next two weeks, and we talked about everything from our kids, our favorite concerts, and the best books we've read to favorite vacations we've taken and playing guitar. We talked about everything but our disease. Maybe it was intentional to keep our conversation light.

When you're newly sober, sometimes the last thing you want to talk about is the disease. Please treat me as you would anyone else and not one slapped with a death sentence. I didn't want people to tiptoe around me, treating me like a piece of china teetering on the edge of a shelf. It wasn't because I was trying to ignore or avoid talking about it, but because my life isn't this disease. My life is many things, and, oh yes, I have this disease too.

It was a breath of fresh air that someone would reach out to me and offer genuine care and complete support, knowing and under-standing what I needed when I needed it and how to give it to me.

Absolutely nothing can be more precious than time spent talking with another recovering alcoholic. They know where you've been, understand where you're going, and instinctively know how to help.

It was a beautiful thing for this relative stranger to keep things so simple for me because my emotional deluge was severe. When the physical withdrawal had finally passed, the floodgates opened, and I was carried downstream in a salty waterway of my tears. When my coping mechanism was gone and the fog of detox in my brain began to clear, I had diagnosed myself as being insane. Life was going on around me, and on the inside, it felt like chaos.

Sixty-One

RIDING THE WAVES

AT FORTY-TWO YEARS OLD, I REALIZED THAT I WAS wholly ill equipped and maladjusted to life. I had absolutely no way to handle anything. I didn't know what I was feeling, why I was feeling it, or what the hell to do about it. I had spent the bulk of my life killing my feelings with alcohol that I had no idea what to do when those buried feelings began to emerge.

I had my coffee friend sitting there telling me that I think too much, which frustrated me to no end. "Yes, you're right. I overthink everything, and that's why I drink," I said.

He put his coffee down. "Yep, you've got that right, my little grasshopper. Welcome to sobriety, kid." I did not feel very welcomed. I couldn't fucking sit still, or those damned *feelings* would creep in and leave me crying.

About a month into being sober the second time around, I began to realize how emotionally stunted of a human being I was. I had no tools in my toolbox to deal with the life that kept coming at me. Every time I'd open it up, loose screws and nails rattled around inside this otherwise empty box. No wonder my life was a mess. I didn't receive the set of tools necessary to be a functional human in this world, and because of it, I had spent most of my life spreading my human wreckage everywhere.

The new sober me was in a constant state of emotional turmoil, which I was unable to control. The relentless waves kept smacking into my body and knocking me over onto what felt like a beach of solid rock. Someone had handed me a piece of paper that listed all of the basic human emotions, and within that list of emotions were descriptions of each. When a feeling came up, I was to refer to my list to see just what it was that I was feeling. I felt ridiculous having to refer to a sheet of paper with human emotions, but that's what I needed to do. I needed to break it down to the basics because it was apparent I didn't even have that.

As ridiculous as that piece of paper was in my hands, it was invaluable. I could identify feelings but had no idea what the underlying feeling truly was. Sure, I was sad. But what *kind* of sad was it? I was happy. But what *kind* of happy? I was angry. But what *kind* of angry was it? By referring to that ridiculous piece of paper, I was able to identify what caused the wave to hit me in the way that it did. I had no idea that so much was involved in feeling because not only had alcohol been killing my anger and sadness, but it had also killed my happiness and joy.

I wanted to get well, so I climbed on top of that surfboard and rode the waves, clutching tight to that piece of paper. Laying on the rocky shore wasn't going to help me get anywhere except being carried back out to sea. My Dad certainly didn't raise me to lay down and drown in my misery, oh no. Whenever I felt I was getting stuck there at the shore, I could hear him yelling, "Get up, get up! Just do it.'

Hearing my dad's voice only served to deepen that inborn stubborn streak in me, so it was natural for me to want to fight this disease just as I had fought everything else in life. Was alcoholism something I could win? Would I be cured if I fought hard enough? Just what did I have to do to get what I wanted?

Sixty-Two

HELLO! ARE YOU LISTENING?

THE ALCOHOLICS I KNOW TEND TO BE STUBBORN AS all get-up. They are unreasonable, illogical, bossy, anal, egotistical, people-pleasing, type A folks who could quite possibly be one split hair away from being serial killers. As much as I loved to believe I was special, I wasn't.

It's no wonder so many of us were seemingly cast out of society, considered to be wastes of life, broken, and lost causes. Often, we sit untreated in jails and holed up in mental hospitals because nobody knows what the heck to do with us otherwise. We are but the helpless, sick stains on society who didn't deserve better until there were people out there who said we did.

Every sick person deserves to get well. I'm not sure why some of us are chosen to make it while others aren't. From my own experience, the ones who make it are the ones who come to believe that they are worth saving. At three months sober, I was still waffling back and forth on that.

Riding the waves of sobriety was no fun, and my paper was getting soggy. Never had I experienced such inner torture by just being alive. I spent most of those first ninety days either just sitting on my hands, so they didn't do anything wrong, or on my hands and knees at 4:00 a.m., scrubbing grout with baking soda and a toothbrush. Since I had put down the bottle, I had gotten back a lot of hours in my day and had no idea what to do with them.

Most of my energy was of the nervous variety, and it made me very squirrely upstairs. When I had energy I didn't know what to do with, I was to pick up the phone and call someone. Sure the house would look like a million bucks, but it would do me no good to run myself into the ground. I had a list of numbers to call, but going back to that stubbornness, I'd take out that list only to shove it back into the drawer thirty seconds later. No way would I swallow my pride and call anyone. If I was struggling, I was just fine struggling on my own, just as I always had.

I liked being alone besides. I was comfortable there. Alone was my safe place where nobody could hurt me, attack me, criticize me, insult me, or otherwise disturb my peace. Why would I pick up the phone and complain about my consequences? I was the one who got myself here, and my self-reliance I had always counted on would get me out. I stuck to the one thing I knew best when things in my head would go haywire: I isolated. Even in a room full of people, I could still isolate myself and often did. People scared me. It was safe to seek out a quiet corner where I could sit peacefully, a glass of wine in my hand, eyes peering down at the plate of food in my lap.

The last couple years of my drinking had been the worst. It was as if I put myself on a remote island somewhere. On the shore was a boat with a hole in it that I had made. The waters surrounding the island were so rough that any thought of rescue was fleeting at best. To spite myself, there was always a feeling that someone was there with me, dragging me through the sand with a patch for my boat and the ability to calm the waters, if I would just get the fuck over myself and let Him help.

Soon I came to realize that there was absolutely nothing I could control except my reactions, isolated or not. It was my first lesson. As much as I didn't want to feel anything, I was powerless to stop it from coming. The only thing I could do was accept that the feeling was there and name it, feel it, honor it, and let it go. Feelings don't kill people.

Sixty-Three

HOPE

I HAD SPENT SO MUCH TIME REACTING AND OVERRE-
acting to things that didn't require a reaction at all. Had I any emotional maturity, I could have avoided most of my problems. Sure,
challenges will always arise, but maybe if I stepped back and got
quiet for a minute instead of playing the what-if game, or trying to
fix things that didn't need fixing, the answers will come and with it
the ability to remain calm. As far as I knew, the only one that could
grant such peace in me was God.

Since getting sober, I had begun to grow accustomed to the ex-
traordinary, and, slowly, things that I had once dismissed as silly
or a waste of time became necessary for me to keep and maintain
some level of sanity. On a frigid fog-shrouded morning in January
2019, I got on my knees and did what was necessary. I surrendered.
Knowing that all else had failed, I turned my life over to God.

Before I could get up off my knees, a warm blanket of peace wrapped itself around me like a father warming his child after being outside in the cold. In my head, I heard a voice breathe a sigh of relief, finally. What took you so long? It wasn't a burning-bush kind of moment, but it felt as if the light of God had entered and lit Himself on fire inside of me. At that moment, I knew that no matter what happened now, everything would be ok. All that *stuff* that happened before was over now, and I didn't have to hold it anymore. After so many falling outs I had with the guy, if I was going to stay sober, God and I would have to become friends again. Not only was He the only form of defense that I had in this world, He was the one still standing next to me when everyone else had bailed in battle.

It was strange to start each day in prayer. I didn't even know how to pray correctly or if there was a way to pray correctly. I always envisioned prayer as a formal to-do with set rules and guidelines you had to follow. Grandma had a bunch memorized and had me recite them along with her. I liked Grandpa's much better. His were always short and to the point. My personal favorite was "Rub a dub dub, thanks for the grub. Yay God!"

The praying I knew came only in times of complete desperation. God, if you keep me from getting sick from these shots of tequila, I swear I'll never drink tequila again. God, please don't let me get pulled over; I don't want a DUI. And my most used prayer: God, please don't let me be pregnant. After years of pleading with the guy to get me out of trouble, I had no idea what to say. So I started with something that I felt was most important: God, please keep me sober today. That wasn't a prayer to bail me out but a prayer for protection from what I might do, and that was a first.

I was told to be patient when praying. I needed to be gentle and comfortable with myself in not knowing and to be ready to accept that my prayers won't always be answered in the way I expect them to. My ego needed to sit in the backseat. As far as I knew, prayers didn't work, and so I felt ridiculous at first.

I mocked people who ate up part of their day with praying. As I saw it, prayer was for those holy-rolling religious folks who couldn't control their own lives, going about it in any way the napkin fell. Prayer was inaction at its finest. I saw it as an easy way out of accepting responsibility or accountability. Prayer was for those who couldn't make things happen.

It didn't take me long to realize that my ideas about prayer were all wrong. Prayer didn't take reservations for the holy people. Prayer was for everyone, and it didn't matter one bit who or what you prayed to as long as the God you were praying to wasn't you. I knew of people who didn't believe in God, and those people sent their prayers up into the universe. Some folks prayed to their houseplants or the trees outside. None of it mattered. The only thing that mattered was an open heart.

My God concept was already there, but I had to tear down everything I knew, toss it out the window, and start to rebuild again at the foundation. I was not going to get anywhere with someone else's vision of God. I tried going back to the God of my childhood, and it only made me resentful. I emptied my head of everyone else's ideas and wrote down the qualities I wanted in my vision of God.

It was then when I started to get excited about God. I put my pen down and looked at my list. It was everything I had ever wanted in another human being but could never find in one person. My

God was now anything and everything that I had ever wanted. With that revelation, my life began to change. The way I saw God now opened all of the doors and windows that I had closed. I still saw myself as a prisoner, but now there were bright and beaming rays of light where all my darkness had been residing. For the very first time in my life, I had hope.

Sixty-Four

SURRENDER

MY LIFE WAS STILL A STEAMING PILE OF GARBAGE, hope or no hope. Things don't just change overnight when you get sober and find God. I may have had both now, but all my wreckage was still there, smoky and smoldering. Whatever good I had remained in a pile of ash at my feet, unrecognizably smoldering.

Everything I had heard about alcoholism was right. In just a few years' time, I had absolutely decimated everything and everyone I had ever loved, and I hadn't a clue how to go about repairing any of it. Some of the things I had done in the throes of my disease were downright reprehensible. Just when I thought I had done the most horrible thing, there was always something worse following behind. There was one thing I was able to do consistently: fuck shit up. I didn't know anyone who could outdrink me, and I didn't know anyone who could make more of a disaster out of things than me.

I did a lot of flying under the radar with my drinking. Things started splendidly then very quickly spiraled out of control. From what I heard, women tend to be worse drunks than men. We get drunk quicker, fall quicker, and meet death quicker than our male counterparts. In my case, it snuck up on me, and by the time I noticed, death was ready to end my story.

A visit to the doctor after my last nine-month bender confirmed it. I had fatty liver disease as a direct result of my excessive liquor consumption. Luckily, it was early enough that it was reversible *if* I stopped drinking; otherwise, it would lead to much more severe issues and, ultimately, death. I had ignored all the warnings of alcoholism being a progressive disease. You don't think anything bad will happen to you until it does. Alcoholism had cost me nearly everything, and now it could very well cost me my life.

I was sober four months before I managed to get myself to the doctor. I was afraid of what she would find. On par with everything else in my life, I figured if I didn't go to the doctor, then nothing would be wrong. "So, tell me about your drinking," she said. Everyone knows when you go to your doctor, you lie about your habits, but seeing as how I quit drinking months ago, I felt like I could admit to what I had done. After all, if I couldn't get honest, my hope was going to find someone else to inspire.

The doctor peered at me from over her glasses. "How many drinks do you consume a week?" I tried to stifle a laugh. Honest, honest, you need to be honest.

"I don't know. I don't keep track." Her eyes widened, looking for me to continue. "After three or four inside an evening, I'd just stop counting, pass out, or black out. Blackouts were the worst." At this point, she was typing rapidly on her computer, so I continued. "Usually in the morning, I'd come to without any recollection of what I did the night before or wound up waking up somewhere I didn't remember going. I drove drunk late at night, and I never knew how I got home. I had hangovers every single day, and the only way I could get rid of them was to drink. Oh, and one more thing. I'm not as bad as my brother. I've never been in legal trouble, at least not yet."

The doctor looked dumbfounded and immediately suggested a ninety-day treatment program.

"Sorry, I can't do that."

Her lips tightened. "I'm sorry? Did you say you can't, or you won't?"

I couldn't go anywhere for ninety days. I have four kids, a husband who works full-time, and no family nearby. Who the heck is going to take care of my kids while I'm gone? I tried to explain, but apparently all she heard was excuses. For once, I was not giving excuses. It was all true.

"Ok. How about an outpatient program?" she asked.

Now that I could do because I had already been doing it every single day for the last four months. "Done deal," I told her.

The doctor's office called a few days later with the results of my blood work: elevated liver enzymes indicating fatty liver disease. "No need to be alarmed as long as you continue to stay sober. The liver will heal itself," she said.

I thought, well, that's a God thing right there. I have a chance. He has given me an opportunity, and I better take it because there may not be any more of them if any at all. My phone rang again just as I hit the end-call button on my phone. It was a friend from the room. Two God moments. I hear you loud and clear.

The voice on the other end of the phone didn't even say hello. My friend started the conversation. "Are you ready to get well?" She was willing to show me how to dig up all my roots, rearrange them, and grow a brand new tree. It would not be easy work, but since I had accepted and invited God's company, I'd come out through the other side with an entirely new way of living. With an offer like that and as desperate as I was, I jumped at the opportunity.

My insides yearned for relief. I needed to let go of it all and hand it over. What's done was done, and there was nothing I could do about that. My past had kept me stuck, frozen inside a time frame I could not see myself out of. I clung to my past like it was a badge of honor. My victimhood was who I was. What would I be like if I took my life back from the years of damage? What if I was something more than just a sum of other people's pain? What if I turned to God and asked Him what He wanted me to be? I'm sure He didn't see me as a victim. He didn't see me as damaged or broken. He saw me as His child. What would He want for His child?

Sixty-Five

PEN TO PAPER

WHATEVER FRIENDS I HAD LEFT AFTER MY LAST blackout disaster began to fall away from my life, and those who did stick around weren't sure how to be around me. They were doing the exact opposite of what I wanted. Of course, my entire life revolved around what I wanted.

Friends adjusted to my new way of life. They filtered things they would have ordinarily said and treated me like a piece of porcelain, afraid that I could crack at any moment. Soon I stopped getting invitations to get-togethers while other *friends* avoided me altogether like I had an infectious disease. There was just one friend who stuck around, and even she didn't know how to act. I didn't have much time for friends anyway now, and most of them were heavy drinkers themselves, so it was reasonably easy to say goodbye without having to say the actual word.

I had taken up with new company now—sober company—and I had a lot of hard work ahead of me. As petrified as I was to get to know these fellow alcoholics, I was eager to soak up their years of wisdom. Every day I brought my leather-bound journal with me and wrote down anything that made sense to me or made me want to consider a different perspective. There were real gems to be had in each day. Someone always had something to say that resonated with me, and soon I became less and less afraid of sharing my story too. It felt like freedom.

The more I immersed myself with these strangers, the easier it became to trust, which is something I hadn't been able to do in a very long time. When you sit in a room full of people who are just like you, it almost feels like home. Had I found my tribe after all those years I had spent looking and never fitting in anywhere? Was my home with these people? The last place on earth I thought I would find my people was in a room full of alcoholics, but once my guard went down and I opened my mind, it all began to make sense.

I took to my recovery as if my life depended on it because it did. I knew that if I went back out again, I would never make it back in. I drove myself over to Office Depot and picked up a stack of legal pads and some fancy pens. If I was going to spend an undetermined amount of time writing, I was going to use the most beautiful pens money could buy. It was finally time to face the demons that made me pick up the drink in the first place. I was ready to turn those glasses around and take a long, hard look at the person looking back at me because, honestly, I had no idea who she was at all.

There were strict orders not to share my writing with anyone. "Under no circumstances are you to share this. You are not to share it with your best friend, your husband, and especially not your kids. Make sure you never leave it lying around. Your writing will be for your eyes and your eyes only." I heeded the warning from my friend. She had been in the room for decades and over some time, we had become extraordinarily close. I trusted her implicitly. Since Grandma, I hadn't allowed any sort of vulnerability with another human being. I had no choice but to trust my friend. With boxing gloves on, my guard remained up just in case.

Besides, I was scared of her. There was something inherently terrifying about her that I couldn't quite understand. It took me some time to realize that I had met my twin. She could see right through my bullshit and would often tell me, "You can't manipulate a manipulator." Well, fuck. I wasn't going to be able to get away with anything with this lady. She was quick to call me out on my excuses and poor behavior and shut down my temper tantrums before they even started. I had met my match.

Alcoholism is a fatal disease, and she reminded me of that every time I'd start dragging my feet. She made damn sure that I knew if I went back out and tried my hand at drinking again, there was a high probability that I'd drink myself to death. So I did every single thing she told me to do. I cemented myself to the belief that only God alone could save me from my alcoholic misery and that intense inner reflection and prayer was the only way to do it.

I took to writing down a list of somewhere around eighty resentments I had been harboring, knowing my very life was at stake. I was scared to death of drinking again and was willing to do anything it took to prevent that from happening. I flipped through my pages and pages full of names and felt ridiculous. Seriously? I had people on my list as far back as when I was three years old that I wanted to hurt just as much as they had hurt me.

At the very top of my list sat Mom and Dad. I had them listed as the people who affected and harmed me the most. They were guilty. I thought that if everyone had to make a list like I was doing, parents would be near the top of them all. Parents will fuck a kid up and not even know they're doing it.

Of course, I learned that not everyone resents their parents. A lot of people have lovely childhoods with stable homes and stable parents. I often marveled at how lucky those people must be to have things so June Cleaver, white-picket-fence perfect. I remember visiting my friends' houses when I was growing up and being jealous of the normalcy I saw. I wondered how people with picture-perfect lives wound up with a seat next to mine in the room. If they didn't have a set of parents to blame for fucking them up, then what was their story?

My eyes would dart around the room, searching people's faces for what caused their lives to crumble like mine. I had a good solid reason, I thought. I knew, however, that their reasons were none of my damn business. I was dissecting my life not theirs.

Sixty-Six

INSIDE OUT

I HIT THAT ROOM FULL OF CRAZIES ABOUT TWELVE times a week in my first six months of sobriety. I had to stay as close as I possibly could. Rumor had it that most people didn't stick around for more than ninety days, and the numbers just continued to drop off from there. That wasn't going to be me. It happened before, and I'd be damned if it was going to happen again.

I was terrified of the woman who was helping me wade through my bullshit. The writing I had to do was taking me forever, but I guess it would since I had so many people to blame for how shitty my life was. Any time I'd call and complain about how long it was taking me to work through my list or how my hand was cramping up, she'd give me a bunch of one-liners that left me more pissed off than I was before I called her. "You can tell me to fuck off, you know," she said. I wouldn't dare.

There was something special about this woman. She could rip me a new asshole and say I love you in the same sentence. I never knew what to do when I hung up the phone. I'd sit there and seethe for a bit, but ultimately I concluded that she was doing what was best for me, which was to tell me the truth. She didn't sugarcoat anything to make things more palatable. One of the hardest and best things she ever taught me is that truth is not hurtful. Truth is loving, and sugarcoating kills people.

I had a lot of support during the time I was writing all my shit down on paper, making it come true. The people in my life gave me space when I asked for it, and when I didn't ask for it, they gave it to me anyway. Years of knowing me gave most people the ability to understand what I needed even when I didn't know myself. My friends, my parents, my husband, and my kids were all on my side. They believed in me and in what I was doing, even if not everyone understood. Even if they bailed, I would always have God. He knew what I was doing and why I was doing it. He understood.

God gave me the strength to face my reality, as ugly as it was. He gave me a hand that I needed to walk into the dark, gather it all up, and walk out to spread it all over the table to say, "Here I am in all of my beautiful mess." He had already forgiven those who victimized me as a young child and had also forgiven me long before I even thought of forgiving myself. Self-forgiveness and complete trust in God's will for me is the end point. My job now is not to get past, or over, what happened. My job is to go through what happened and come out the other side with a fresh set of eyes and a new way of life.

God or no God, drunks drink and runners run. It's just what we do, and sometimes finding something that will keep you sober is a downright terrifying thing. It's not uncommon for alcoholics to dry up for a while, only to go back out there with the rest of the world when things start to get tough. It's far too easy to fall back on what we know, especially when it comes to that dreaded word *accountability*. Nobody enjoys putting themselves under a microscope, particularly us alcoholics.

I didn't want to perform surgery on myself and expose all those moving parts that had spent so much time crashing and banging around inside my seemingly empty shell. It was a mess in there. It clanged around so much inside that my moving parts had parts themselves. Everything had mutated and multiplied in their madness. Sure, I could open it all up on my own and try to deal with it, but it was far more comforting to know that I didn't have to do it alone. Before I sobered up, it was much easier to go through life drinking than to go without, and now I was finding it much easier to go through sobriety with God than alone.

Even with God, I still found room to complain, because the ego is a hard thing to kill. Day after day, I bitched and moaned about how daunting of a task this self-examination was, but there was no way around it. I had to disassemble to resurrect and rebuild to recover. Differences of opinion on how much time I should be spending on myself weighed me down, but I was doing my best to keep one foot in front of the other and take the punches as they came.

I wrote for four months. My fingers calloused up, pen after beautiful pen ran out of ink, and I was walking around wearing the insides of my body draped all over my outsides. No longer was anything in secret. It was all written down now in good old black and white. There was no more hiding, no more running, and no more blaming. I served my time inside my prison, and now parole was coming.

Sixty-Seven

OUTSIDE IN

AS I FLIPPED THROUGH DECADES' WORTH OF PAIN, two things were abundantly clear: At some point in my life, very early on, I was a victim, and that God had not once turned his back on me. I had turned my back on Him. I had cut myself off from the sunlight of the Spirit by playing a victim of circumstance in scenes I created and directed.

There was a time that I had no voice or a choice in any of what happened. Maybe if I had stayed upstairs in my warm little bed, I wouldn't have witnessed my young mother cowering in fear of my father's unbridled rage, but I had an instinct to try and save her. She needed protecting, and I'm not sure what I could have done at three years old, but it was instinct. It was my mom; I loved her, and I didn't want to see her cry.

Even at such a young, tender age, love propels us to do things even if it's scary. Though I wondered where God was as my dad destroyed our house, He *was* there. Not only did my mother and I continue to go on after that terrifying night, but I can look back now and realize how much love I had inside of me. It was as if I was born with the capacity to love, and that sure as heck didn't come out of anywhere. That night with my father was supposed to happen, for it taught me just how resilient and loving I could be, even in the face of fear.

I claim no responsibility for the violence in my childhood home any more than I can claim responsibility for what happened to me at Sunday school, and I undoubtedly cannot blame my mother for how she reacted. That boy at Sunday school had no right to abuse me sexually. No child deserves abuse in any form. It's not right, and it shouldn't happen, but it does. Abuse begets abuse, and if that fifteen-year-old boy was sexually abusing a five-year-old little girl, I could only imagine what had happened to him.

My poor mother probably had no idea what to do when I told her, and she probably handled it the best way she knew how at the time. You have no idea what people are going through, what their stories are, or how to fix something that seems unfixable. You put one foot in front of the other and do the best you can at the moment. My mother was probably terrified, distressed, and at a loss as to what to do. Things were different back then. Sexual abuse, like alcoholism, just wasn't something that anyone ever mentioned. It happened, and you carried on as if it didn't because it was safer that way.

As for my idea that God failed to protect me in His house, that was a misguided belief. I thought if He defended me anywhere, it would be inside a church where we go to worship Him. Instead of blaming God, I can ask myself what God was trying to teach me, and in that case, the lesson was compassion. I am not the only one hurting. That boy was in a labyrinth of his pain, and I was but an outward symbol of his inner torture. He, too, was a victim just as much as I was. Today, I hope he has found his peace, knowing that he also may have turned his life over to alcohol or drugs to cope with his trauma.

Traumas are tragic things, and they repeat themselves unless and until their victims muster up the courage to face them and turn their experiences into teaching tools for others. Where I once stood in a blanket of shame, I hold my head high and use my bad for good. My traumas serve a purpose. They make me uniquely designed to help someone else. I can either choose to repeat the cycle, or I can change my perspective and share my story so that anyone who may be going through what I went through can see that they, too, can survive what's happened to them. There's something very empowering when someone can say, "Yes, me too," because when those words come tumbling out of your body, you realize that you're not alone anymore.

Having a trauma is like being cut in one spot over and over again. The scar gets thicker and thicker until nothing can change its appearance. Instead of leaving that scar alone, it gets picked at in all sorts of ways and never heals. I picked at mine by running into the arms of boys, strangers, and one-night stands. Anyone who showed me even an ounce of love, I pushed away and closed off, deeming myself unworthy of anything good because of that one initial cut.

While other people had played their parts in the story of my life, I took their actions to the extreme. I acted out and destroyed myself over words that I believed to be true. I never once stopped to think that what happened to me was a direct projection of what happened to them. I failed to understand that their path in life was handpicked by God, just as mine was.

Everyone, alcoholic or not, was just as sick as me in some respect. We are all just human beings trying to do the very best we can. When I turned off the microscope and pulled out the slide, the only thing I saw was me. I was to blame for my mess. I was the drunk, and everyone else was but a victim of my ego.

Sixty-Eight

THE IMPORTANCE OF FRIENDS

I WROTE UNTIL MY INSIDES SPILLED OUT AND THERE was nothing left inside of me but an empty shell. I spread my broken puzzle pieces out all over the table and moved them around with my bare hands. I was raw, every scab picked over, and I was bleeding.

The people closest to me had no idea what to do about me any more than I did. Something wasn't quite right about me, and everyone around me once again began to walk on eggshells as if I'd crack at any moment, and that one final crack would send me clear over the edge. This time I wasn't drunk. I had begun the arduous process of healing, and with it comes an enormous, indescribable shift in personality. I was changing, but the only person who couldn't see it was me. Whereas everyone was telling me they were witnessing a caterpillar spin itself into a cocoon, I felt crazy, absolutely unequivocally insane.

I continued to stay very close to my room of nuts. If they were happily sober, I believed I could eventually get there too. Where once I couldn't fathom not ever being able to have a drink again, other ideas had begun to take shape. Maybe if I work through all of this *stuff* and finally rid myself of these self-imposed chains, I won't *have* to drink again. If I got rid of the poison, I wouldn't have to drink the poison. I was all in.

I found myself gravitating to a handful of people who seemed to have exactly what I wanted. They were generally happy people, and when things did go wrong in their lives, they still seemed to be ok with it. None of them flipped out or handwrote invitations to pity parties. They rarely complained or postulated that the world was against them. They seemed to accept that life is what it is, and that the only thing that was in their control was their reactions. My friends didn't sit there seething in anger, plotting revenge. They acknowledged their anger, got to the root of why it was there, addressed it, and moved on. I wanted to know how to do that because my emotions ran my life.

There was something else striking about this new batch of people of mine. Waking up in a strange man's bed after a blackout wasn't something that shocked them. They didn't bat an eye when I said that I used to drive drunk or manipulate people to get what I wanted. My new friends could relate to those mornings of waking up in strange places, not knowing how you wound up there. They had been there too. They had hurt also, and they had been angry, too, but they knew a better way now. My new clan of misfits took my hand and promised there was hope and happiness on the other side of my disease, and they would happily help me get there.

"You're not going to vaporize, you know. I know it's tough shit you've been working through, but it's not going to hurt you to read it out loud. I promise," said the guy who had black coffee coursing through his veins. He had a way about him that always felt like a passive-aggressive slap to the face, but I liked it. He hadn't had a drop of alcohol in over thirty years. People don't get that kind of sobriety just by waking up in the morning. He and countless others ran into the fire, filled with their own special brand of fear, emerging from the flames carrying buckets to save people like me.

For a while, I didn't want anything to do with anyone in that fire. I had it in my head that everyone was looney, like it was a bad thing. Maybe they were looney, but I was too. It was up to me to find my unique brand of crazy. The ones who would nod their heads and softly mumble "me too" would be the place I would call home.

Although I didn't go into the room in search of any friends, it seemed like I was making them in spite of myself. I went in to get sober, and my new crew was a side effect. Soon, they became the oxygen my lungs needed to breathe.

For months, I went in and out of the room, flashing a smile, nodding my head, trying not to make contact with anyone. God forbid I get roped into a conversation. Sure, we had similar stories, but I didn't know any of these people, and the only thing I hated more than large crowds were small ones. In large groups, it was easier to disappear and blend among the vast rolling sea of faces. But in a room of ten people, there was nowhere to hide. The only thing that would make me comfortable in this situation was a drink, and that was totally off the table here.